Guide to Biblical Coins

Guide to
Biblical Coins

David Hendin
with values by Herbert Kreindler

NEW YORK
AMPHORA BOOKS
1987

Copyright © 1987 by David Hendin. All rights reserved

ISBN: 0-88687-328-2
Library of Congress Catalog Card Number: 87-070484

First edition.

Amphora Books

15 White Birch Dr.
Dix Hills, New York

Printed in the United States of America

*For my father, Dr. Aaron Hendin,
who taught me the real value
of the coins described herein.*

CONTENTS

INTRODUCTION

How did I get interested in collecting ancient Biblical coins? It is the question I am most often asked. So here's the story.

In 1967, just after my college graduation, I went to Israel in response to the nation's request for volunteers to fill civilian jobs of young men and women who served in the Six Day War and its aftermath. I started my year as a volunteer in an *ulpan,* or language school, in Beer Sheba. I had never been a voracious reader in high school or college, but the pace at the language school was rather slow, so I began to read a lot. I think I started with Max Dimont's fascinating *Jews, God, and History,* and went on from there. I read several books a week, and eventually the local English bookstore didn't have much more for me to read.

In those days I used to visit Jerusalem often on the weekends. I loved the sights, sounds, and smells of that city. From the first moment that I saw the pink Jerusalem stone of the ancient walled city, I felt I belonged there. On one visit to the Old City, I decided to buy a gift for my dad— a long-time collector of ancient coins, especially coins of Jewish significance. I wandered the narrow streets of Old Jerusalem until I found a shop that seemed to sell ancient objects. I remember the entrance courtyard, filled with hundreds of ancient pottery jars and other mysteriously interesting objects. I was welcomed into the shop by a short, wiry Arab wearing a white knitted skullcap, not unlike a Jewish yarmulka. I asked about ancient coins and was shown a lot of them, none of which made any sense to me. Some of them were expensive, and on my volunteer's wages I couldn't afford much. Finally, I settled on a generous handful of "uncleaned" small bronze coins that the shopowner said needed to be spruced up and attributed. There must have been 100 or more coins, and they cost ten dollars. I put them in a sack and took them back to my room in Beer Sheba, where I put them under my bed, hoping I'd remember to send them home. I promptly forgot about them. Several weeks later, on a visit to the bookstore, the manager touted me on a new book in English called *Guide to Jewish Coins of the Second Temple Period,* by Ya'akov Meshorer. I flipped through the book and noticed photographs of a coin that I thought I had seen in my handful. The curiosity was too great: I bought the book and brought it home to read. Before long I was carefully sorting through that handful of coins with a magnifying glass, and that was the beginning of my own collection. I never did send those coins to my dad, but the pleasure of discovering a hobby he had known for years was reward enough for both of us.

Over the years I have learned not to wax too eloquent about my interest in ancient coins, for the eyes of even one's closest friends glaze over quickly. Some people just can't begin to understand the fascination ancient coins can hold.

I hope that this little book will be of interest to both collectors and nonspecialists, since it does more than describe the coins, but brings them into the fascinating history of our civilization. This new volume incorporates all of my previous book, *Guide to Ancient Jewish Coins,* while significantly updating and expanding its contents. The reader will also note that I have gone to some lengths to avoid renumbering. Feedback from hundreds of collectors over the years has convinced me that the last thing anyone needs is yet another set of numbers attached to the coins. For this reason I have also included an expanded conversion table between the most popular current references in the field (Appendix A).

The earliest known mention of money in the Bible is in the Old Testament story of Abraham. Among other items it speaks of silver with regard to the covenant of circumcision. Later in this same story we read the word "shekel," when Abraham purchases the cave of the Machpelah for a family burial site. However, in this context the shekel must be considered a weight rather than a coin, since coins as we know them were not invented until much later, about 700 B.C.E. Those weights are discussed in an early chapter of this book.

One word for money, "pecuniary", comes from the Latin *pecus,* or ox. This is derived because one talent was the weight of gold needed to purchase an ox. And "shekel" is the Babylonian word for one one-hundredth of a talent.

The first coins were simply small lumps of metal marked in some way. This mark was meant for the one who did the marking; if the same lump came back to him he could recognize it and avoid reweighing, thus speeding up the transaction. From this system the first true coins developed, probably in Lydia, where the king put his own marks on the metal lumps, thus guaranteeing their value. As time passed the crude marks became designs which were stamped onto the metal. (Even prior to this, however, people in China were using odd-shaped pieces of metal as coins.)

Information and Acknowledgments

The reader should note that in the catalog of the coins, the legends sometimes vary slightly among the sketches, the photographs, and the descriptions. This can occur for several reasons. First, of course, there are minor varieties of each of the coins, and sometimes the engraver made spelling or engraving mistakes. Second, especially with regard to the city coins, most of the plates are taken from DeSaulcy, which was published in the 1800s. Sometimes the only specimen available of a particular coin was in very bad condition, particularly around the edges, where the legend appears. Thus the legend was misread, or misinterpreted. This problem continues today with certain coins.

The weights and sizes given are for specimens either in the author's collection or from known references. They are offered as general guidelines, since both size and weight of ancient coins can vary from coin to coin, the silver coins usually varying less than the bronze.

The abbreviations used in designating dates follow Israeli tradition. B.C.E (before the common era) is equivalent to B.C. and C.E. (of the common era) is equivalent to A.D.

Following this section are a few words about the pricing of the coins by Herb Kreindler, an experienced dealer in ancient Jewish coins. The prices given are those that a collector might expect to pay a dealer for similar coins, *not* the prices a dealer would be expected to pay for the coins.

This book does not represent an offering of any coins: it is merely a guide, to be used and supplemented as needed or desired by collectors or students.

The author is indebted to many numismatists who have written important works on Jewish numismatics and ancient history that have been referred to in compiling this volume. Some of them are listed in the bibliography. It should be noted that these scholars deserve most of the credit; I have done mainly a journalist's job of sifting, merging, cutting, and clarifying the information.

Before acknowledging the many friends who have been of major help with this project, I would like to mention two good people who have died since my first book on this subject was published: Nasrallah Sahuri, a lover of antiquity, was murdered; Meyer Rosenberger, expert tailor, extraordinary collector and scholar of city coins, lived a full life and left a legacy of knowledge for all of us.

Thanks to these friends who have helped me develop my interest in ancient Biblical coins: G. Momjian, David Jesselsohn, Leo Dardarian, Harvey Hoffer, Joe Rose, Ed Janis, Fred Jacobs, Bob Schonwalter, Rafi Brown, Menasha Landman, Y. Zadok, Leo Mildenberg, and others I may have forgotten to mention.

Ya'akov Meshorer is a fine teacher, and I have learned more from him in some hours than others could have taught in weeks. Another great scholar, teacher, and friend is Shraga Qedar, with whom I have shared many adventures. Special thanks, too, to Don Simon, Ira Goldberg, Italo Vecchi, and Herb Kreindler, all of whom have spent valuable time reviewing and commenting on sections of the manuscript for this book. Their assistance notwithstanding, any factual or other errors herein are the author's responsibility.

My wife, Jeannie, has helped and encouraged this project, as have my children Sarah and Benjamin. Benjamin helped photograph the coins.

As mentioned earlier, Dr. Aaron Hendin, my father, first sparked my interest in ancient coins. Some background information for this introduction was taken from his manuscript "Jewish History as Portrayed on Coins," which was partially published in the *Shekel*.

My father ended his short essay with these words: "To hold in one's hand a coin of the brave Maccabees or the hated Romans helps one transcend time and space and be more akin to our ancestors of old as well as our Israeli brethren of today."

Those words only begin to describe the fascination of the ancient coins of the Bible days. Each has been protected by the parched Israeli climate for some 2,000 years and then brought to light and given new life, not as a coin of the realm, but as a key to the mind. The doors this key can open will be limited only by your imagination.

P.O. Box 805   DAVID HENDIN
Nyack, NY 10960   APRIL 1987

A WORD ABOUT THE VALUATION GUIDE

The intention of the pricing guide is to give the collector relative dollar values of the coins in very fine condition covered in this guide. The prices are based on conservative grading standards and cover the last five years of auction and private sales. The principal change from the last guide is the change to VF for all coins, reflecting the increase in availability of quality material in this series.

The values represent the opinion of the cataloguer, and comparable coins may sell for more or less depending upon market conditions and demand at the time. Coins in better grades, particularly the bronzes, will bring significantly higher prices if they are well centered with full legends and devices. This is important to remember: a common coin of Agrippa I, no. 75, for example, might sell for $20 in very good (VG) condition. A specimen in fine (F) condition might sell for $40, but the same type of coin in very fine (VF) or better condition, well centered and well struck on both sides, with a beautiful patina, could bring $150 or more.

Note that most of the coins pictured in the plates are far superior in condition to the coins priced; thus the plates are meant to illustrate the coin types only, and not to approximate coins that might sell for the prices indicated.

No representation is made in this book either to buy or to sell at the prices listed herein.

HERBERT KREINDLER
NEW YORK, MARCH 1987

1. COLLECTING BIBLE COINS

The Thrill of the Hunt

In a small limestone hut in an Arab village on the West Bank of the Jordan River, not far from the ancient city of Hebron, several men sit on squat stools and drink from tiny cups of sweet tea with peppermint sprigs or strong, sweet Turkish coffee with aromatic spices.

Our host (we shall call him Abu Yusif, meaning "Father of Joseph"), wearing traditional Arab robes and a *kefeiah,* has already served us several courses of snacks, including fresh local fruit and a sweet, sticky, yellow, fried pastry. Now it is time to see the main course—but it isn't going to be more to eat.

Abu Yusif leaves the room and returns shortly carrying a dirty red bandana tied in a bundle. He places it casually on the low table and, slowly, begins to tug at the knots.

I lean forward in anticipation and catch the pungent, musty smell of the cloth. It has been buried for safekeeping, perhaps in the yard, or under one of the loose tiles that cover the dirt floor of Abu Yusif's home.

Inside the bandana are nearly 100 bronze and silver coins. Some of them are separately wrapped in carefully knotted plastic bags or tiny envelopes. The newest of these coins was issued in the ancient land of Israel more than 1,800 years ago. The coins are worth scores of thousands of dollars.

The first time I saw valuable coins in the hands of an Arab villager, I rubbed my hands together in greedy delight. I dreamed of buying them for a fraction of their true market value and putting them into my collection, or trading duplicates with other collectors for a tidy profit.

Alas, my bubble of naiveté was quickly burst. Many Arab villagers who deal in ancient coins and other antiquities know the international market very well. Once, in the corner of a poverty-stricken, one-room hut, I saw a cardboard carton filled with recent European auction catalogues.

On this day, I slowly examine Abu Yusif's coins and select a small group of them. Now negotiations begin in earnest. The bargaining is serious. In the tourist markets, buyers and sellers play a kind of game. The shopkeepers only allow themselves to be bargained down to the correct retail prices—though they will have no complaint for the eager tourist who is willing to pay more.

But when one deals with people who have found the material they are selling, there is room for real bargaining. Here, too, the doctrine of *caveat emptor* is vital. The best American and European dealers guarantee coins to be genuine. When buying from the source, each person must be his or her own expert.

After nearly two hours, I buy six coins from Abu Yusif. Four of them will go into my own collection. I have bought the other two for the permanent collection of The Jewish Museum in New York, where I helped to prepare an exhibition called "Coins Reveal," showing coins and medals related to ancient and modern Israel.

The man in charge of The Jewish Museum exhibition was Israeli archaeologist and coin expert Dr. Ya'akov Meshorer, then in the United States on a sabbatical. He is a professor of archaeology at Hebrew University in Jerusalem, and has been curator of numismatics at The Israel Museum since it opened in 1965.

A native-born Israeli, Meshorer can trace his direct ancestors back at least seven generations in the Jerusalem area. He grew up in a land where true collectors find coins in the soil instead of on trays in dealers' shops.

Meshorer's dark eyes sparkle when he talks of the many places in and around Jerusalem where the soil and climatic conditions are such that ancient coins are often perfectly preserved for the lucky finder. When he was a first-year college student, he used to walk from the bus to Hebrew University, looking for coins as he went. One day, on a hill called Gi'vat Ram, he found a silver coin of Athens, struck in the sixth century B.C.E. To this date it is the oldest coin ever found in Israel.

Meshorer enjoys telling another story: "When we were children, my twin brother and I used to find a lot of coins in a courtyard near our home. They were really beautiful coins. We later found out that somebody who lived in a building next to this courtyard had a collection of coins. Every time his little sister got angry with him, she would throw some of his coins out of the window. These were the coins we were finding. We had to give all of them back."

Once, as Meshorer took a visitor on a tour of The Israel Museum's exhibits, he paused before a glass case containing a small pottery oil lamp and a pile of small bronze coins. He motioned toward the display and told about the 1964 excavations of the ancient settlement of Ein-Gedi, on the shore of the Dead Sea, where a house from the first century C.E. had been preserved almost to its original height.

While archaeologists were taking pictures, one of the workers accidentally knocked a piece of plaster off a high portion of the wall, thus revealing the ancient clay oil lamp containing 139 small bronze coins (called prutot or quadrantes), issued mainly by the Roman procurators who ruled Judaea under Rome between 6 and 66 C.E. Meshorer concluded that these 139 coins could not have been a hoard in the usual sense, since their value was so small that one would not salt them away for the sake of saving or hiding money. At any rate, since the coins were hidden behind the plaster in the wall of the house, it was unlikely that the owner ever intended to recover them. So the archaeologist reconstructed the events leading up to the hiding of the coins as follows:

"A Jew in the year 60 C.E. built his house, and, while finishing it, before its last plaster stage, decided to hide a sacred amount of money in the wall to protect against the evil eye."

Was it pure chance that there were 139 coins? Or was there a reason for this number? Meshorer has the answer:

In ancient times, the most sacred sum of money to the Jews was the half-shekel, since this was the amount each person paid as the annual tribute to the Temple. But, according to Meshorer, our first-century Jew did not want simply to put a single, silver half-shekel into his wall for luck since "the large number of coins apparently would make a better impression." The man also decided to put the money into a lamp—"a symbol of eternity," Meshorer notes.

But wait. Half a shekel was equal to only 128 of the small bronze coins. So why were there 139?

Deduces the archaeologist: "One who came to the Temple to donate his tribute of half a shekel and gave it in different currency (other than the usual silver currency of the city of Tyre, then officially and exclusively used for this purpose) to be changed by the money changers . . . had to add a sum equal to eight percent of the tribute."

That fee was the same kind of fee banks charge today for converting one nation's currency to another's. And eight percent of 128 is almost 11, "thus putting in the lamp 139 quadrantes, making the exact holy sum of half a shekel, in small change."

This is only one example of the kind of fascinating detective work in which a numismatist or archaeologist can engage.

The True Collector

I've always been surprised to find people who want to collect coins, but don't want to learn anything about them. Do you remember the syndrome of collecting mainly to fill the holes in your penny, nickel, or dime collection?

I'm reminded of the time I spoke before a group of people, most of whom collected coins of modern Israel. As my talk proceeded it became obvious that I could both read and write the ancient Hebrew language that appears on ancient Jewish coins. And there was an exclamation of surprise: "How did he ever learn to do that?" one fellow asked.

As I recall it, my friend Ed Janis, said, "He learned it while you were out hunting for a Seafaring commemorative!"

This anecdote, then, raises a good question. Why do we collect? Not only ancient coins, but modern and medieval, or even tokens and medals.

To be sure, there are many reasons to collect coins. Among them are fun, investment, and knowledge. A true collector is driven by the force of all of these, plus more. It is not easy to explain the thrill of collecting to one who is not a collector. Many avid collectors would liken their continuing search for coins to the "thrill of the hunt." Believe me, when one finds a particular coin for which he has searched for many years, it can be as exciting as bagging big game in Africa.

I have never understood those who want to collect coins but don't care about learning the history behind them. They often want nothing more out of their coin collections than to fill the blank spaces in a book, or to complete a set of numbers in a catalogue. I have met hundreds of people who strive to fill those blanks, but who are turned off when it comes to making an effort to learn anything about the coins that are filling the spaces. Yet this may be the most pleasurable aspect of coin collecting.

It is, for example, impossible to have a full appreciation of the coins of modern Israel without knowing something about the coins of ancient Israel after which they are patterned. And it is a shame to collect the coins of ancient Israel without understanding the history of the Jewish and Christian religions right up to the modern day. Of course, the background and history of the Bible—both Old Testament and New—are also important; this is only one of many resources on the subject. (See the bibliography for additional reading.)

How Ancient Coins Are Dated

Many persons—including coin collectors—have never given the dating of coins much thought, and thus are surprised to find that the methods we use to date coins today are relatively modern as far as numismatics goes.

In fact, the first coins using the current dating system were not struck until 1234 C.E. by the Roskilde mint, now in Denmark. By that time coins had been minted for more than 1500 years. Many of those earlier coins had dates, but they were not dates as we know them today. Ancient coins were dated by the regnal year of the ruler or by a local era. This would be the equivalent of dating 1977 coins of the United States "Year One," corresponding to "The first year of the rule of Jimmy Carter."

The first dated Jewish coins were apparently struck under Alexander Jannaeus, King of Israel from 103 to 76 B.C.E. Not all of his coins were dated, but at least one type was. This is the small bronze (see coin number 12) that carries on its obverse an upside-down anchor within a circle surrounded by the Greek for "of King Alexander." The reverse shows a star of eight rays surrounded by dots and a crude Aramaic inscription, which translates to "King Alexander Year 25."

On the obverse, many specimens of this type have a number of dots at the points of the anchor. These are meant to spell out the letters L KE in a style almost identical to the lettering on Seleucid coins of the same period. These letters no doubt also signify the date, Year 25, referring to the 25th year of the reign of Jannaeus—78 B.C.E.

Some of the coins of Herod I are dated L Γ, referring to the official third year of Herod's reign, or 37 B.C.E. (Herod actually reigned from 37 to 4 B.C.E., but he had been officially designated "King of Judaea" by the Roman Senate and Octavian in 40 B.C.E.) However, it was three years before he could wrest the throne from Mattathias Antigonus, last of the Hasmonean kings.

The coins of the First Jewish War Against Rome are dated from "Year One" to "Year Five," which correspond to the five years of the war: 66 through 70 C.E. The coins of the first year are quite rare, and those of the fifth year are exceedingly rare, with only about a dozen of them known.

During the Bar Kochba War (132–135 C.E.) the coins were dated "Year One" and "Year Two." A large number of the Bar Kochba coins are not dated, but evidence from the study of die combinations, breaks, and wear shows that the undated coins were undoubtedly issued during the third and final year of the war, 134–135 C.E.

How Ancient Coins Were Made

It is worth discussing some interesting aspects of the minting of coins in ancient times, particularly the coins of the ancient land of Israel. Actually, methods of striking coins have changed remarkably little, except, of course, those changes due to improved metallurgy and technology.

The blanks, or flans, for the Judaean bronze coins were made by casting metal in molds consisting of shallow, round sockets connected by channels drilled into pieces of soft limestone. (One researcher believes that these limestone molds were actually used to cast wax, which was, in turn, used to mold cast the coin blanks.) After pouring molten metal into the molds and letting it cool, strips of coin blanks connected by short metal ribbons were removed. These are called flan strips. An assistant would reheat each strip and then place the first blank flan in between two striking dies on a sturdy base, perhaps a tree trunk. The moneyer hit the top die with a hammer, thus striking the coin. Then the assistant pulled the strip one coin further, and the process was repeated.

This process was obviously carried out fairly quickly, and the resultant coins were struck off center more frequently than not. After striking, the flan strip was chopped apart into coins and the remaining metal scraps were melted down once again.

PLATE A shows a bronze flan that escaped striking and has been preserved as an ancient "slug" for thousands of years.

Sometimes the man in charge of chopping the coins apart didn't do a very good job, resulting in coins with long projections from one or both sides, such as the coin of Alexander Jannaeus shown in PLATE B. Also note that many of the other coins shown in the plates have obvious flat edges where they were chopped away from the flan strip.

Occasionally, the flan strip broke, one flan becoming stuck in the lower die (or vice versa) after striking. When the next flan was inserted and struck, it received the full strike from the top die, but instead of receiving the impression from the bottom die, it received instead the face of a coin that had already been struck by the top die. This caused the design of the top die to be impressed *in incuse* on the reverse of the coin. The Hasmonean coin shown in PLATE C resulted from such a mistake. Its obverse shows the usual anchor, but the reverse shows the exact design struck in incuse, like a negative.

Yet another minting error common in ancient times was double striking. PLATE D shows the reverse of a coin of Agrippa I that has been struck twice. The resultant design shows three ears of barley pointing upward and three ears struck across them.

Sometimes the dies used for striking coins cracked or broke. Usually one or more coins were struck with the damaged die before it was discovered and replaced. PLATE E shows the obverse of a coin of Hyrcanus II with a very obvious crack right down the center of the die.

All of these minting errors are interesting because of what they can teach us about the ancient methods of making coins. They are commonly encountered in the ancient Jewish coins, and any collector with a sharp eye can find them for sale.

What Are Barbaric Coins?

We are often asked about coins that are referred to as "barbaric," or those that are said to have "retrograde" inscriptions.

Barbaric coins are those that are usually crude in the alloy, the striking, the design and cutting of the dies, or a combination of all these factors.

Retrograde inscriptions are those that appear in "mirror-image writing" instead of the normal form.

There is lively discussion among numismatists concerning the coins in these categories. We are especially interested in them because they occur frequently in many types of ancient Jewish coins.

It has been said, for example, that the very barbaric coins of the First Jewish War Against Rome (66–70 C.E.), as well as those of the Bar Kochba War (132–135 C.E.), were struck by Jewish soldiers hiding out in the Judaean Hills.

Ya'akov Meshorer writes that "Because of the unstable position of the Jewish administration, and the lack of a central mint, the mint masters were often changed. Occasionally, unskilled people prepared the dies, and not only do the coins with the barbaric designs reveal bad style and obvious lack of skill, but also, they indicate work done under the pressures of the time limitations."

This is a rather fascinating possibility, since collectors would no doubt favor these coins if this were their origin.

To our knowledge there have been no metallurgical analyses of this series. Such tests could determine whether the alloy of the barbaric coins differed significantly from the alloy of the normal series. If it did so on a fairly frequent basis, it seems quite possible that the barbaric coins were indeed minted under "field" rather than "mint" conditions.

On the other hand, it is equally possible that the barbaric Judaean coins were struck in the central mint by either poor craftsmen or apprentices who made errors.

This theory has some support in the fact that in addition to barbaric coins of both revolts, there also exist barbaric coins of the Hasmoneans, the Herodians, and the Procurators of Judaea.

Retrograde inscriptions cannot be used to support either theory specifically. The retrograde inscriptions probably occurred because the individual cutting the die was inexperienced. He did not understand the principle of die-making that necessitates the cutting of the die in reverse. When the "negative" die strikes the metal, a true image is formed.

As beginners, engravers worked by copying. Thus they probably cut their first dies by copying prototype coins and not other dies. When coins were stamped from those dies, the inscriptions appeared in retrograde.

We don't know if the dies for the retrograde coins were engraved by beginning diemakers in the mint, or with rebel bands of Jews hiding in the hills.

Leo Mildenberg writes that "the artisans who produced the irregular bronze dies were not only mere copyists imitating regular dies and even irregular works, but also unskilled copyists. For, their craft is inexpert, their hand insecure and their understanding of the legends, and even single letters, poor or entirely absent. The overall picture of their production is entirely different from the surprising achievement of the men who cut the regular bronze dies."

Another common irregularity that occurs especially on the Hasmonean coins, even those that are not barbaric or irregular, is the misspelling of the words in the ancient Hebrew inscriptions.

Scholars account for the errors in this way: The ancient Hebrew script was already out of use at the time the Hasmonean coins were issued (beginning about 100 B.C.E.). Many of the people never learned it; they had to go to libraries and consult old manuscripts to see what the letters looked like.

Most people in those days were not literate. It is very possible that even skilled craftsmen such as die engravers were not literate, and certainly not in ancient Hebrew. The primitive form of writing had already been replaced by the currently used Aramaic alphabet.

Thus craftsmen engraved the inscriptions by copying letters that meant nothing to them from a design onto a die. If you don't think that's difficult, try copying a few words in Chinese without making errors. Thus the frequent misspellings on the Hasmonean coins can also be explained.

Fakes and Forgeries

Show me a serious collector of ancient coins who says he (or she) has never unwittingly bought an altered or outright forged coin, and I'll show you a naive collector—or a person telling a fib.

There are many forged or altered coins, and the coinage of ancient Israel is not immune from this plague. Indeed, because of the high degree of interest in ancient Biblical coins, there may be more replicas in this field than in others.

Replicas made by American museums in recent years have the word COPY stamped on them, according to current United States law. But many false coins are not stamped. I once saw an entire "collection" made up of common forgeries of ancient Biblical coins. Each of the forgeries had been battered, retoned, or dipped in acids to make it look ancient.

The authenticity of some coins is controversial. It is not unusual to find two experts who disagree as to whether a particular coins is genuine. Once I bought from a reputable dealer a large bronze coin of Vespasian with a "Judaea Capta" reverse.

When I showed it to a friend, *he thought it was fake.* I took it to a man in New York who is said to be one of the best experts on ancient Roman bronze coins. *He said it was fake.*

The next time I visited Washington, D.C., I showed the coin to a curator at the Smithsonian Institution. *He said it was genuine.*

Finally, I had the coin sent to the curator of ancient coins at the British Museum in London. The report came back that he had carefully examined the coin and he was certain it was genuine.

"The coin does have a slightly cast appearance," wrote the British Museum curator, "but this is probably due to the fact that it may have been found at the bottom of the River Tiber."

Aside from outright forgery, there is the matter of retooling coins. This is especially dangerous in the larger bronze coins, but I have seen cases in which the tiniest Jewish bronze coins have been carefully tooled to raise the relief of the coin, or even to change the legend altogether.

On the other hand, sometimes a coin is mechanically cleaned simply to remove encrustation or patina, and the actual bronze of the coin is not really cut into. Sometimes it is difficult to tell exactly what has been done to a coin, if anything.

Here are some points from an excellent checklist that appears in the book *Selections from the Numismatist on Ancient and Medieval Coins:*

—"Examine the coin for general appearance.

—"Examine the coin with a hand lens. Does the edge show signs of joining? Are there any file or hammer marks present around the edge or around the dotted borders? (Hammer marks are expected on the Jewish silver coins of the First and Second revolts; indeed, if they are missing, the coins must be suspect.) Are pockmarks of casting present on the surfaces?

—"Examine the legend carefully. Do the letters show signs of "tooling" or other forms of alteration?

—"Does the patina on bronze coins appear to be genuine?" (This is a valuable guide, but remember that large numbers of ancient bronze coins are found in a condition that necessitates cleaning and eventual retoning of the coin. Some collectors refuse to buy coins that have been cleaned. Such coins do not bother me as long as they have been cleaned lightly and carefully.)

—"Is the coin the proper size and weight of similar coins of the period? Frequently forgeries will be too heavy or too light by a considerable amount."

Final warning: Purchase ancient coins from reputable dealers who stand behind their sales.

If you are not satisfied with a coin's authenticity, check it with an expert in the field. The extra time will be well worth your while, and will save future disappointment for yourself, or your heirs.

Cleaning Ancient Coins

Unlike modern coins, a great number of ancient coins *must* be cleaned. Since these coins lie in the ground for 1,000 years or more before they are found, they often acquire a thick layer of encrustation which must sometimes be removed before the coin can even be identified.

It is not easy to remove such an encrustation safely; this is a job for experts. The best restorers of ancient coins work with steel needles under a binocular microscope, and remove the encrustation physically. Sometimes chemical cleaning is the only alternative.

On the other hand, some types of oxidation are extremely desirable on ancient coins, and should *never* be removed. Such oxidation is called patina. Patina is the thin layer of material that often forms on the surfaces of bronze coins after long contact with desirable combinations of atmosphere, soil, moisture, or other factors. The patina can form in various colors, ranging from red or orange to deep jade green. Ancient bronze or copper coins with a uniform jade-green patina are worth many times more than coins without such a patina.

Dr. Arie Kindler, director of Israel's Kadman Numismatic Museum, has written that for the purpose of cleaning, ancient coins may be divided into three main categories:

1. *Worn*—that is, rubbed down so that cleaning would be of no value at all.

2. *Covered with a delicate patina*—which, if it does not prevent the reading of the legend or cover the design, would only suffer through cleaning, and, therefore, no such steps should be taken.

3. *Covered with a thick layer of dirt and corrosion*—but with the possibility still remaining that cleaning would reveal enough to identify the coin and leave it in reasonable condition.

As stated above, the cleaning of ancient coins, both bronze and silver, is a task best left to the expert conservator in this field.

Nevertheless, it is my experience that collectors of ancient coins will at least once get the urge to buy a corroded and encrusted coin and try to clean it up in the hope it will be of value. I have seen coins cleaned by methods ranging from brushing with an abrasive toothpaste for many hours to scrubbing with steel wool. These cleaning methods are generally not effective, since they can do more harm than good.

Here is some advice from Dr. Kindler on cleaning ancient coins chemically:

"The solution of the chemical bath consists of one part sulphuric acid to nine parts distilled water. The coin is left in the solution for several hours, by which process the patina is dissolved, as well as the dirt. The coin is then removed from the acid and brushed with a fingernail brush to remove the brown material that has formed on its surface. If dirt still remains on the coin, the process is repeated. If, after the coin has under-gone this process four times, it is still not clean, a new solution should be prepared. To remove all traces of the acid, the coin is left in distilled water for two weeks, the water being changed every day. Upon being removed from the distilled water, the coin is to be washed in soap and hot water, no brush being used."

The Coin Plague

To be distinguished from the deep-green, stable patina many ancient bronze coins acquire is the light-green, powdery deposit known as coin plague. This "plague" can grow rapidly over an entire collection of ancient bronze coins, especially if they are not stored properly. Coin plague is caused by humidity combined with harmful, usually acidic, substances, either on the coin or in the air. (There is *no* bacterial factor to this "disease," so ster-ilization is of no value.) I have seen a collection that was supposedly "healthy" only weeks before develop this condition on many of its coins.

To prevent coin plague from the outset, make sure that your coins are kept in a clean, dry place. Coin plague can spread, so if you find the green speckles "growing" on one of your coins, remove it from the rest of the collection immediately.

Here is Dr. Ya'akov Meshorer's method of curing a coin of the coin plague.

With a splinter of wood, a toothpick, or a bristle toothbrush, carefully scrape away as much of the green material as possible.

Then begin soaking the coin in a glass of distilled water. In very serious cases you may add a small amount of soap to the water.

Change the water, rinsing the coin and the glass every two days. Keep repeating this process for at least three weeks, even if the plague seems to have disappeared sooner.

When the process is finished, dry the coin with a cloth, then place it under the bulb of a desk lamp for several hours so it becomes thoroughly dry.

You may then spray the coin with a uniform, thin coat of a flat-finish lacquer, which you can buy at an art-supply store.

If over a period of time the plague returns to this coin—it should not if you have followed the above instructions carefully—you can remove the lacquer with thinner and repeat the entire process.

This method is effective only if coin plague affects just the surface of a coin. If the plague has penetrated to the core of the coin, it is unlikely that any home-treatment method will save it. If this has happened to a particularly valuable coin in your collection, I suggest you contact an ar-chaeology expert from either a local museum or a university for advice on who will be able to help you preserve this coin properly. Don't be surprised to find that a professional conservator may charge a *minimum* of $150 per coin for treatment.

2. A TIME BEFORE COINS

There were no coins in ancient Israel during the days of the First Temple (960–586 B.C.E.). This fact is confirmed by the complete absence of coins in the extensive archaeological excavations which date to that time and earlier.

Before coins were invented barter was the method of trade. One early and popular commodity was cattle, mentioned when Abraham asked Abimelech to be a witness to his digging of a well of Beersheba:

> And Abraham set seven ewe-lambs of the flock by themselves. (Genesis 21:28)

Barter also played a critical role when Joseph acquired all of the land of Egypt from the people on behalf of Pharaoh during the years of famine:

> Buy us and our land for bread, and we and our land will be bondmen unto Pharoah. (Genesis 47:19)

Elsewhere in Genesis, Abraham is described as having been

> very rich in cattle, in silver, and in gold. (Genesis 13:2)

Abraham lived during a time of transition from the nomadic life to one of settlement. As a practical matter, the transition from the use of livestock and other commodities as items of barter to the use of precious metals also occurred at about this time.

Although precious metals were being used in trade, Old Testament references to specific coins of the First Temple period are anachronistic, because the historians who put the Bible into writing lived in later times, when coins of silver and gold *were* commonly used. Thus these writers incorrectly assumed that coins had been used during the earlier periods as well.

A statement in the first book of Chronicles, written during the Persian Period (539–333 B.C.E.), after coins had been invented, shows the writer's confusion in describing a transaction that took place in an earlier time. He refers to both coins and weights of metals when discussing the contribution of gold darics toward the building of King Solomon's Temple:

> And they gave for the service of the house of God of gold five thousand talents and ten thousand darics, and of silver ten thousand talents, and of brass eighteen thousand talents, and of iron a hundred thousand talents. (I Chronicles 29:7)

In ancient times the relative values of various metals—gold, silver, and bronze—were set by general agreement, often based on the price of a head of livestock. Thus the specific and relative weights of metals were important, and a reasonably accurate system of weights developed.

Different ancient cultures, however, had different weight standards. Hence the Canaanite-Israelite system probably was different from the Mesopotamian system and others. There is some support for this in the Old Testament, which mentions at least three kinds of shekels (emphasis added):

> And Abraham weighed to Ephron . . . *four hundred shekels of silver,* current money with the merchant. (Genesis 23:16)
> *This they shall give, every one that passeth among them that are numbered, half a shekel* after the shekel of the sanctuary. (Exodus 30:13)
> *He weighed the hair of his head at two hundred shekels,* after the king's weight. (II Samuel 14:26)

Next to the shekel, another important weight in Biblical times was the talent. A few lines from Exodus (38:25–26) explain the relationship between the shekel and the talent:

> *And the silver of them that were numbered of the congregation was a hundred talents, and a thousand seven hundred and three score and fifteen [1,775] shekels, after the shekel of the sanctuary: a beka a head, that is, half a shekel, after the shekel of the sanctuary, for every one that passed over to them that are numbered, from twenty years old and upward, for six hundred thousand and three thousand and five hundred and fifty [603,550] men.*

In other words, 603,550 men each gave a half-shekel to the congregation—301,775 shekels in all. These 301,775 shekels were equal to 100 talents plus 1,775 shekels. Thus 100 talents equaled 300,000 shekels, and one talent of silver was equal to 3,000 shekels.

Another unit of weight mentioned in the Bible is the *mina,* which is equal to about 50 or 60 shekels. The Akkadian mina was equal to 60 shekels, but there is reason to believe that the Canaanite-Israelite mina equaled only 50 shekels.

The first mention of money in the Bible occurs during the story of the covenant between God and Abraham:

> *He that is born in thy house, and he that is bought with thy money, must needs be circumcised . . .* (Genesis 17:13)

The Hebrew word for money actually used here is *kesef,* which means silver, probably referring to an ingot of silver. Later in Genesis we learn just how that silver is measured when we read about Abraham buying the cave of the Machpelah from Ephron the Hittite for the burial of his family:

Abraham weighed to Ephron the silver, which he had named in the hearing of the children of Heth, four hundred shekels of silver, current money with the merchant. So the field of Ephron, which was in Machpelah . . . and the cave which was therein . . . were made sure unto Abraham for a possession of a burying-place. (Genesis 23:15–20)

If these "shekels of silver" had been coins there would have been no reason to weigh them during the transaction. Both Literary and archaeological evidence tell us that the precious metals of Old Testament days were probably in the form of ingots or jewelry, cast in various sizes for ease in handling:

The man took a golden ring of half a shekel weight, and two bracelets for her hands of ten shekels weight of gold . . . (Genesis 24:22)

The importance of weighing precious metals during a business transaction is stressed many times in the Old Testament:

And I bought the field that was in Anathoth of Hanamel mine uncle's son and weighed him the money, even seventeen shekels of silver. And I subscribed the deed, and sealed it, and called witnesses, and weighed him the money in the balances. (Jeremiah 32:9–10)

In ancient times, as today, there were apparently a significant number of scoundrels who figured they could cheat in business transactions by keeping two sets of weights—a light and a heavy—in their bags. One was for selling, the other for buying!

Thus we are warned:

Just balances, just weights, a just ephah [a unit of dry measure], and a just hin [a unit of liquid measure], shall ye have. (Leviticus 19:36)

**Using ring weights in ancient Egypt.
Detail from a Tomb in Thebes
c. 1400 B.C.E.**

And warned again:

> *Thou shalt not have in thy bag diverse weights, a great and a small.*
> (Deuteronomy 25:13)

The Prophets, too, expressed repeated concern over the problem of dishonest merchants:

> *As for the trafficker, the balances of deceit are in his hand.* (Hosea 12:8)
> *Making the ephah small, and the shekel great, and falsifying the balances of deceit.* (Amos 8:5)
> *Shall I be pure with wicked balances, And with a bag of deceitful weights?* (Micah 6:11)

The shekel, most commonly used everyday weight in the days of the Old Testament, was divided into several fractions.
The *beka,* or half shekel:

> *A beka a head, that is, half a shekel, after the shekel of the sanctuary.* (Exodus 38:26)

The *pim,* or two-thirds of a shekel:

> *And the price of the filing was a pim.* (I Samuel 13:21)

The third-shekel:

> *Also we made ordinances for us, to charge ourselves yearly with the third part of a shekel for the service of the house of our God.* (Nehemiah 10:33)

The quarter-shekel, or rebah, was suggested as a gift from Saul to Samuel the prophet:

> *And the servant answered Saul again, and said: "Behold, I have in my hand the fourth part of a shekel of silver, that will I give to the man of God, to tell us our way."* (I Samuel 9:8)

The gerah was one-twentieth of a shekel. In Akkadian the word *gerah* means "a grain of carob seed," which probably matched its small size:

> *This they shall give, every one that passeth among them that are numbered, half a shekel after the shekel of the sanctuary—the shekel is twenty gerahs—half a shekel for an offering to the Lord.* (Exodus 30:13)

Archaeologists have discovered many kinds of ancient weights in Israel, and they serve to confirm what the Bible tells us about these denominations.

Some of the weights actually carry inscriptions, but most of them are blank. One type of these weights is dome-shaped and carved from stone. If marked, the inscriptions were incised on the top of the dome, and the weights have flat bottoms so they would not roll off the scales. Various inscribed weights, including forty shekels, eight shekels, four shekels, two shekels, one shekel, *beka,* and *pim* have been discovered. Another inscribed Jewish weight, the *netsf,* five-sixths of a shekel, also has been discovered.

Of course the Israelite weight system was not the only one in the Holy Land in ancient times. Other systems existed before and after, and yet others existed in places near and far at the same time. This is comparable to the pound system being used in some countries while the decimal system is used in others. Even today, deep in the markets of cities like Jerusalem, Hebron, and Bethelehem, one can see Bedouin women weighing fruits or vegetables using a rock of a particular size to balance their scales.

Many collectors of Bible coins also become interested in ancient weights, since these small weights were frequently used in monetary transactions— the weighing of silver or gold or other precious commodities. Thus we describe some general types of weights from each of several periods as they are relevant to the Holy Land up through Arabic rule. Tables also show the relative weights and the average gram weights for the known denominations. The weight tables are provided by Shraga Qedar.

Syrian-Phoenician Weights, 15th to 11th centuries B.C.E.

Weights from this period are often made of hematite and shaped like elongated barrels with flat bottoms to prevent rolling. Sometimes bronze weights of similar shape, often with rings on one end, are found. The rings were added or removed to make the weights more accurate. The famous hematite Babylonian duck weights are from this period. Duck weights are shaped like floating ducks with their heads turned back, resting on the backs of their bodies. The duck weights are usually pierced.

Babylonian Weight Table for Syrian-Phoenician Weights

MANÛ	516.00 g	1	
SHIQLU	8.60 g	60	1
3 REBUTI	6.45 g	80	1⅓
½ SHIQLI	4.30 g	120	2
SHALASHU	2.86 g	180	3
REBUTU	2.15 g	240	4
KHUMMUSHU	1.72 g	300	5
SHUDDU	1.43 g	360	6

PITQU	1.07 g	480	8
KHALLURU	0.86 g	600	10
GIRÛ	0.36 g	1440	24

Egyptian Weights, 11th to 9th centuries B.C.E.

Egyptian weights were often made in the form of bronze animals such as frogs, ducks, lions, bulls, and even fish and houseflies. Many Egyptian weights in the shape of small cupcakes also exist; they are usually made of bronze or diorite.

Egyptian Weight Table

SEP	940.00 g	1		
DEBEN	94.00 g	10	1	
QEDET	9.40 g	100	10	1

Judaean Weights, 9th to 7th centuries B.C.E.

The most common type of Judaean weights were described earlier in this chapter: they are the dome-top, flat-bottom polished limestone weights. They are often found without inscriptions; those with inscriptions are much rarer.

Judaean Weight Table

		Weight	I	II	III	IV	V
I	Talent	34.2 kg	1				
II	Mine	570.00 g	60	1			
III	Shekel	11.40 g	3000	50	1		
IV	Beka	5.70 g	6000	100	2	1	
V	Gerah	0.57 g	60000	1000	20	10	1

Phoenician Weights, 4th to 3rd centuries B.C.E.

Flat-topped bronze blocks, which taper inward on all four sides, are the most common weights for this period. These weights often carry crude symbols inscribed on the base.

Phoenician Weight Table

MINE	1			
SHEKEL, STATER	50	1		
½ STATER	100	2	1	
⅟₁₆ STATER	800	16	8	1

Stater weights: 370–358 B.C.E. = 12.85 g
                     358–332 B.C.E. = 10.80 g
                     332–275 B.C.E. = 8.63 g

Roman Weights, 1st century B.C.E. to 5th century C.E.

A large variety of lead and bronze weights exist from this period. The lead weights are mainly flat and of a geometric shape, often carrying a design or inscription, or both. The bronze weights are often barrel-shaped and carry an inscription etched (or inlaid) on the top.

Roman Weight Table

LIBRA	360.00 g	1							
UNCIA	30.00 g	12	1						
SICILICUS	7.50 g	48	4	1					
SEXTULA	5.00 g	72	6	1½	1				
DRACHME	3.75 g	96	8	2	1⅓	1			
SCRIPULUM	1.25 g	288	24	6	4	3	1		
OBOL	0.625 g	576	48	12	8	6	2	1	

Byzantine Weights, 5th to 7th centuries C.E.

Occasionally, Byzantine or late Roman bronze coins were inscribed and used as weights. Most often, however, the weights of this period were flat bronze disks or squares with the weight value clearly inscribed on the top.

Byzantine Weight Table

LIBRA (ΛΙΤΡΑ)	324.00 g	1		
UNCIA (ΟΥΓΓΙΑ)	27.00 g	12	1	
NUMISMA (ΕΞΑΓΙΟΥ)	4.50 g	72	6	1

DRACHME (ΔΡΑΧΜΗ)	3.375 g	96	8	1⅓	1			
SCRIPULUM (ΓΡΑΜΜΑ)	1.125 g	288	24	4	3	1		
OBOLUS (ΟΒΟΛΟC)	0.563 g	576	48	8	6	2	1	
SILIQUA (ΚΕΡΑΤΙΟΥ)	0.188 g	1728	144	24	18	6	3	1

Arabic Weights, 7th to 12th centuries C.E.

Faceted bronze spheres are the most attractive weights from this period, and this particular type apparently was issued and used from the beginning of the Arabic period, which replaced the Byzantine era. Flat bronze disks and squares are sometimes inscribed with Arabic names or phrases ("Allah is Great"). Stamped glass disks were also used as weights for much of this period, and they are often found in the marketplace today.

*Arabic Weight Table**

RATL	324.00 g	1					
UQIYA	27.00 g	12	1				
MITQAL, DINAR	4.50 g	72	6	1			
DIRHAM	3.00 g	108	9	1½	1		
QIRAT	0.188 g	1728	144	24	16	1	
HABBA	0.047 g	6912	576	96	64	4	1

*Average values in a period of continuously declining weight standards.

3. PERSIAN THROUGH HELLENISTIC TIMES

In 538 B.C.E., Cyrus, King of Persia, who had already conquered Babylon, allowed the Israelite exiles living there to return to Israel, which was also part of the Persian Empire from the sixth to the fourth centuries B.C.E. Persia's rule ended with Alexander the Great's victory in 332 B.C.E.

During the Persian period coins were used and struck for the first time in the land of Israel. These first Jewish coins basically imitated the coins of Athens, but carried Hebrew inscriptions of "Yehud" or "Yehudah," the Aramaic name for the Persian Satrapy of Judaea. An interesting Jewish addition to these coins was the lily, a characteristic design of Jewish art at the time, and a motif often used in the Temple's decor.

One of these "Yehud" coins depicts on the obverse a bearded male divinity, naked above the waist, but draped below. He sits on a winged wheel, and a hawk is seated on his extended left hand. In the right field is a bald-headed mask. Above the divinity is the three-letter inscription YHD ("Yehud"). Some people believe that this figure depicts the Jewish God as visualized by the Persians. Ezekial's description of the divine chariot may have influenced them:

> And when the cherubim went, the wheels went beside them; and when the cherubim lifted up their wings to mount up from the earth, the same wheels also turned not from beside them.   (Ezekial 10:16)

In 331 B.C.E., Alexander the Great defeated the Persians at Arbela, and his distinctive coinage based on gold staters and silver drachms soon became common in ancient Israel. The famous tetradrachm of Alexander carried on its obverse the magnificent head of Herakles, possibly in Alexander's likeness, wearing a lion skin, and on the reverse a half-naked Zeus seated on a throne holding both an eagle and a sceptre. Some of Alexander's coins were struck at his mint in the city of Akko.

Alexander died in 323 B.C.E., and a number of wars among his generals followed. Shortly thereafter Alexander's empire in the area of ancient Israel was divided between the Seleucids in the north and the Ptolemies in the south.

Thus the third century B.C.E. saw the land of ancient Israel under the rule of the Ptolemies of Egypt. Josephus reports how Ptolemy I Soter (323–283 B.C.E.) captured Jerusalem on a Sabbath, when the Jews refused to fight in their own defense.

At this time the ancient land of Israel was important both politically and economically. It was a strategic land, not only commanding great stretches of the coast, but serving as a crossroads to the entire area.

Under Ptolemy II Philadelphus (283–245 B.C.E.), relations flourished between his capital at Alexandria and the center of the Jewish community at Jerusalem. Philadelphus freed many of the Jewish slaves who had been captured during his father's military campaigns in ancient Israel.

But the best-remembered achievement of Ptolemy II was a literary one. During his reign, the Bible was translated into Greek. Ptolemy II had a large and splendid library, of which he was especially proud. One day, legend has it, the royal librarian told him that he had gathered together 995 books of the best literature that all nations had to offer. However, the librarian added, the greatest books of all, the five books of Moses, were not included.

With that, Ptolemy II sent envoys bearing gifts to the high priest in Jerusalem. The envoys were to ask not only for copies of the five books of Moses, but for a group of scholars to translate them into Greek.

The high priest met the request and sent 72 scholars to Alexandria. It is said that each of them worked alone to complete the difficult and un-precedented task. When they were finished and the translations were com-pared, each of the 72 is said to have been identical. Thus this Greek translation of the Bible was called the *Septuagint* or "the seventy." Now the wisdom of the Jewish nation was available for the first time to others, including those Jews who had been born and raised outside their homeland, as in Alexandria, and had already lost fluency in the Hebrew language.

During the century or so that ancient Israel was under the rule of the Ptolemies, many Ptolemaic coins circulated in the area. They were minted in Egypt, Phoenecia, and other surrounding areas as well as at the local mints of Gaza, Akko, Ascalon, and Jaffa.

Also at this time, a significant series of tiny silver coins was minted, perhaps in or near Jerusalem, by local municipal authorities. These are miniature versions of the silver Ptolemaic tetradrachms, and depict on their obverse the head of Ptolemy I and on the reverse an eagle with the in-scription "Yehuda," which may refer specifically to the city of Jerusalem.

The Yehud Coins

As recently as 1966, Meshorer's *Jewish Coins of the Second Temple Period* listed only four types of the tiny Yehud coins of the Persian period. The Ptolemaic Yehud coins were totally unknown at that time.

In the early 1970s many more types of these coins were discovered and publicized. In 1979 Leo Mildenberg published a comprehensive article that illustrated 28 different varieties of the Yehud coins.

Mildenberg assigned the Yehud coins to three basic periods: under Per-sian rule, during the Macedonian occupation, and in the Ptolemaic King-dom.

In his 1982 book *Ancient Jewish Coinage,* Meshorer essentially agrees with Mildenberg's classifications, although he disagrees on certain points, including the coins Mildenberg thinks were issued during the Macedonian occupation.

It's no wonder experts disagree about these tiny coins. Almost every year since 1970, new examples and types have been discovered. It is something of a mystery why they were discovered at this time and not earlier, since they have been lying in the ground for more than 2,000 years. It is possible that the villagers have simply been paying more attention because of the commercial market. Meshorer writes that "Most specimens were discovered within the borders of the ancient kingdom of Judaea by peasants anxious to meet the increasing demands of the market for ancient coins."

A few of the tiny coins have been found in archaeological excavations in Jerusalem and the surrounding area. However, the vast majority of them have come from the commercial marketplace. Arnold Spaer, a noted Jerusalem attorney and authority on ancient Jewish coins, wrote that almost all of the tiny Yehud coins "seem to have come from the area south of Jerusalem, and more particularly from the Bethlehem district, both east and west of the main road from Jerusalem to Hebron." Meshorer confirms that "One rumor suggests that peasants exploring in an area near the southern border of Jerusalem discovered several of these minute coins by merely sifting the dirt."

At the present, it is simply unknown where these tiny coins were minted, but the Jerusalem area does seem to be a good possibility.

Because the Yehud coins are so tiny, they are often struck so that none of the letters, or only one or two of the letters, are visible. These are valuable specimens, but those with full inscriptions command the highest premium because of their great rarity.

Coins of the Persian Period (before 333 B.C.E.)

1.   AR 8.5mm, 0.35gm.
      O: Falcon with wings spread, head right; inscription in ancient Hebrew above right (Yehud).
      R: Lily. AJC I, 116, 8.   1,750.00

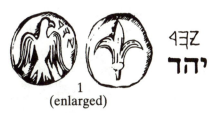

1
(enlarged)

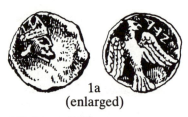

1a
(enlarged)

1a.   AR 7mm, 0.32gm.
O: Head of Persian king wearing kidaris (crown) facing right.
R: Falcon with wings spread, head turned to right; inscription in
ancient Hebrew on right (Yehud). AJC I, 116, 9.   1,250.00

יהד

(enlarged)

2.   AR 7mm, 0.39gm.
O: Head of Athena to right.
R: Owl standing to right, head facing, small lily above left; inscription in ancient Hebrew on right (Yehud). AJC I, 115, 4.
1,000.00

2a.   AR 7mm, 0.515gm.
O: Head of Athena with headdress of three pointed leaves to right.
R: Owl stands to right, head facing front; lily flower to left, inscription in ancient Hebrew on right (Yehud). AJC I, 115, 2.
1,000.00

3.   AR 8mm, 0.23gm.
O: Facing head in circle.
R: Owl standing to right, head facing; inscription in ancient Hebrew
on left (Hapecha—the governor), on right (Yehezqio—Hezekiah). AJC I, 116, 10.   1,500.00

3a.   AR 7–7.5mm, 0.28gm.
O: Young male head to left.
R: Forepart of winged lynx to left, inscription in ancient Hebrew
below and to right (Yehezqio—Hezekiah). AJC I, 116, 12.
2,500.00

יחזקיה
הפחה

3
(enlarged)

3a
(enlarged)

Meshorer places this type in the same period as coin number 3 above, while Mildenberg believes it dates to the Macedonian occupation.

The individual mentioned on the coins is possibly the same Hezekiah mentioned by Josephus in Against Apion (22). Josephus, quoting Hecateus, tells us:

> *"Ptolemy [I] got possession of the places in Syria after that battle at Gaza; and many, when they heard of Ptolemy's moderation and humanity, went along with him to Egypt, and were willing to assist him in his affairs; one of which was Hezekiah, the high priest of the Jews, a man of about sixty-six years of age, and in great dignity among his own people."*

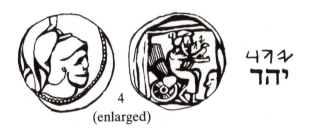

(enlarged)

4.   AR 15mm, 3.29gm.
      O: Bearded head right wearing crested helmet.
      R: Deity seated right on winged wheel, holding falcon in left hand, small mask below right; inscription in Aramaic above (Yehud), all in incuse square. AJC I, 115, 1.   Unique.

Coins of the Hellenistic Period (after 333 B.C.E.)

5.   AR 7mm, 0.177gm.
      O: Diademed bust right of Ptolemy I.
      R: Eagle with wings spread, half turned to left and standing upon thunderbolt; inscription in ancient Hebrew on left (Yehudah). AJC I, 117, 16.   800.00

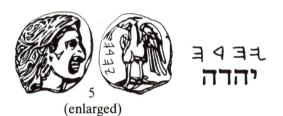

(enlarged)

5a
(enlarged)

5a.   AR 7mm, 0.19gm.
      O: Diademed head of Ptolemy I to right.
      R: Head of Berenike I to right; inscription in ancient Hebrew on
      right (Yehud). AJC I, 117, 15.   1,250.00

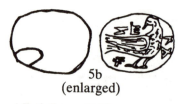

5b
(enlarged)

5b.   AR 6–7mm, 0.31gm.
      O: Pellet. (On other specimens with designs resembling human or
      animal heads).
      R: Bird stands to right, head turned back; surrounded by ancient
      Hebrew inscription (Yehudah). AJC I, 117, 17b.   800.00

4. HASMONEAN COINS

Seleucid Coin of Jerusalem Struck Under John Hyrcanus I

Antiochus son of King Demetrius sent a letter from overseas to Simon the high priest and ethnarch of the Jews, and to the whole nation. (I Maccabees 15:1)

Until the middle of the twentieth century, it was widely believed that the first Maccabean (also called Hasmonean) coins were struck while Simon Maccabee was high priest. Simon died in 134 B.C.E.

This theory was largely connected to parts of a letter that King Antiochus VII (138–129 B.C.E.) wrote to Simon. The king enumerated a number of privileges to Simon, which he offered in order to enlist Jewish support for Antiochus's struggle against Tryphon for the Syrian throne. He said, in part:

I give thee leave also to coin money for they country with thine own stamp and as concerning Jerusalem and the sanctuary, let them be free . . .
(I Maccabees 15:6)

However, archaeological evidence uncovered in the 1950s and 1960s from Massada, Jerusalem, and elsewhere, made it clear that the coins previously attributed to Simon were, in fact, coins of the Jewish War Against Rome (66–70 C.E.), also called the First Revolt.

Perhaps not so incidentally, the Book of Maccabees indicates that once assured of his victory over Tryphon, within a few months after he wrote his letter to Simon, Antiochus withdrew the privileges.

Simon's son and successor, John Hyrcanus I, reigned from 135 to 104 B.C.E. It was apparently under Hyrcanus I that the first coins were issued under Jewish direction. These small coins carried the lily of Jerusalem on one side and the Seleucid anchor on the other. They are found primarily in Judaea, and it is widely assumed that they were issued in Jerusalem mainly for Jewish use. It's worth noting, too, that there is no evidence that other Seleucid coins were issued in Jerusalem, especially those with portraits of the Seleucid kings, as those which were issued in Gaza, Ascalon, Akko, and other cities in the area.

This, apparently, was part of a Seleucid effort at appeasement toward the Jews, whose law stated:

Thou shalt not make unto thee a graven image, nor any manner of likeness, of any thing that is in heaven above, or that is in the earth beneath, or that is in the water under the earth. (Exodus 20:4)

All of this is logical in light of the assumption that one of the early coins of Alexander Jannaeus was copied from the Antiochus/Hyrcanus coin of the lily/anchor type (see coin no. 7). Also note the similarity in style of inscription, as well as the placement of the date on this coin as compared to no. 12.

Seleucid Coin Linked to Judaea

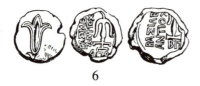

6

6.   AE 14–15mm. Antiochus VII (Sidetes).
O: Anchor upside down flanked by inscription in three lines, ΒΑΣΙΛΕΩΣ/ΑΝΤΙΟΧΟΥ/ΕΥΕΡΓΕΤΟΥ (of King Antiochus, Benefactor), date below anchor ΑΠΡ (Year 181) or ΒΠΡ (Year 182).
R: Lily. Struck 130–132 B.C.E. Kindler 3; AJC I, 160, 1–3.   50.00

Alexander Jannaeus (Yehonatan), 103 to 76 B.C.E.

And now the king's wife loosed the king's brethren, and made Alexander king, who appeared both elder in age, and more moderate in his temper than the rest.   (Josephus, *Wars,* I, IV:1)

Alexander Jannaeus, great-nephew of the folk hero Judah Maccabee, became ruler of the Jews in 103 B.C.E. upon the death of his brother, Judah Aristobulus I. Not only did he become high priest, he assumed the title "king" as well, and for the first time the ruler of the Jews had equal rank with rulers of the Hellenistic world.

The young king was an ambitious warrior, hungry for battle and conquest, and his reign was prosperous, if bloody. Early in his rule he managed to gain control of the entire coast of Palestine, from Mount Carmel in the north, to Egypt in the south, with the exception of Ascalon (Ashkelon), which escaped his armies because of the city's strong ties with Ptolemaic Egypt. Jannaeus's kingdom was roughly the same size as that ruled by King David.

The second decade of Jannaeus's reign was fraught with internal strife in Judaea. Jannaeus had surrounded himself with opulence and grandeur; his Hellenization and militarism deeply disturbed many of his countrymen, particularly the Pharisees, who devoutly believed the laws of the Torah must carefully be obeyed, and thought Jannaeus was neglecting his sacred duties. In short, they didn't want a Hellenized warrior—and one who obviously enjoyed this role—as high priest.

On one occasion his enemies embarrassed Jannaeus by pelting him with fruit while he officiated over the Feast of the Tabernacles in the Temple. The king retaliated by having several hundred of the rebels killed. Civil war raged in Judaea for six years beginning about 95 B.C.E.; some 50,000 Jews perished, according to some accounts.

The opposition among the king's own people encouraged his enemies. In 89 B.C.E., Demetrius III of Syria attempted an invasion of Judaea and defeated Jannaeus near Shechem (Neapolis). This setback, however, re-united the Jews somewhat and the renewed unity gave them the power to drive Demetrius out of Palestine.

Toward the end of his reign, Josephus reports, Jannaeus became ill from heavy drinking, which ultimately led to his death. But before the king died he apparently was involved in something of a reconciliation with the Phar-isees. One bronze coin (see no. 17) provides some interesting numismatic evidence of such a truce.

The coins of Jannaeus are probably the most common of all ancient Jewish coins. They carry designs of anchors, stars, cornucopias, lily flowers, and, in one instance, a palm branch. The inscriptions are in Greek, Ara-maic, and Hebrew, the latter frequently containing errors. Some numis-matists and archaeologists explain these mistakes by noting that even as early as Jannaeus's time the ancient Hebraic characters had already given way to the modern Hebrew (Aramaic) script we know today. Thus scribes and engravers had to copy from old scrolls and manuscripts in the libraries; since they were unfamiliar with the ancient alphabet, they made many mistakes.

Of special interest is coin no. 12, apparently the only dated Hasmonean coin.

The Lead Pieces

An important enigma of Jewish numismatics focuses on a coin of Alexander Jannaeus (103–76 B.C.E) that was struck in lead (no. 9).

The lead pieces were mentioned in 1854 by DeSaulcy in the earliest known scholarly work on the coins of the Jews. In 1967 Meshorer wrote that he knew of only about 20 examples of the lead issue: "Their most notable feature is that they are not *proper* coins, for in most instances they were either struck on one side only, or have an uncertain strike on the other side, or several one on top of the other on the obverse and reverse making it difficult to distinguish the precise design. They all share the same characteristics in that they are more suggestive of trial strikings than of actual coins."

In 1974 Arie Kindler observed that the Jannaeus lead coins "seem to have been issued for only a short period during some temporary economic crisis."

Since 1967 there has been an increase in the knowledge of ancient Jewish numismatics. A major reason for this has been the opening of Judaea and Samaria to Israeli numismatists and archaeologists. Here are a few points regarding the Jannaeus lead pieces deduced from knowledge acquired since 1967:

1. Although they remain scarce, the lead issues are no longer as rare as was once believed. Several small hoards have been found, and I have examined more than 200 specimens.

2. It seems clear that none of the lead issues was actually uniface. However, the reverse inscription is often off center or weakly struck. Nevertheless, careful examination of most of the lead issues will show traces of one or more letters or part of the border of dots encircling it.

3. A number of die varieties of the lead pieces have been found, which indicates there were probably quite a large number originally issued.

The questions raised are twofold: First, when were the lead pieces issued? Second, why this unusual issue?

The answer to the first question can be traced to a 1968 article by J. Naveh, in which he deciphered the reverse inscription of the so-called wretched coins of Jannaeus. These are the small, crude bronzes (see coin no. 12) with anchor obverse and star reverse.

Naveh showed that the reverse inscription was in Aramaic, translated as: "King Alexander, Year 25." This twenty-fifth year of Jannaeus's reign corresponds with 78 B.C.E. This is relevant to our study of the lead pieces because they, too, carry a similar Aramaic inscription on their reverse: "King Alexander."

Epigraphically the legends on the lead and bronze issues are similar. Since these are the only two issues of Jannaeus that carry Aramaic inscriptions, it can be concluded that they were struck at about the same time.

To find clues to the motivation for the lead pieces, we must therefore take a look at what was happening in about the year 78 B.C.E. Not many years before (circa 90 to 85 B.C.E.), a bloody civil war had raged in Judaea. It has stemmed from rivalry between the Saducees, the party supporting the king and his Hellenized ways, and the more traditional Pharisees. One can be certain that ill will did not end with the war, but continued for several years thereafter.

Jannaeus died in 76 B.C.E., but it is known that for several years before his death he adopted a more benevolent policy toward the rival Pharisees. One of the concessions he apparently made was to have overstruck a group of coins to eliminate the designation "King" in both Hebrew and Greek, and replace it with the traditionally more acceptable title "High Priest" (see coin no. 17). Further, on the same coins Jannaeus modified the Hebrew spelling of his name from "Yehonatan" to "Yonatan," thus breaking up the combination of Hebrew letters (YEHO-) used commonly as an abbreviation of the Lord's name.

During this period it is quite possible that Jannaeus wanted to initiate further goodwill between himself and the Pharisees. One way of doing this would have been to offer some gifts to the people. This was not unusual in ancient times. The Roman emperors often issued special tokens to be redeemed for food or other commodities. Often these tokens, sometimes referred to as *tesserae,* were made of lead.

Since the language of the masses during the time of Jannaeus was Aramaic, it is not far-fetched to conclude that the lead issues in question were actually tokens issued by the Jewish king to the masses to be redeemed for a gift of food or other commodities.

Thus the lead pieces issued by Alexander Jannaeus in about 78 B.C.E. are possibly the first Jewish tokens ever issued. They remind us of a time when the Jewish nation was ruled by royalty. These tokens are also a reminder that even to a powerful monarch, the will of his people was important enough to warrant significant consideration.

When Jannaeus was succeeded by his queen, Salome Alexandra, power was concentrated in the hands of the Pharisees. Perhaps Jannaeus's concessions and good will toward the Pharisees paved the way for this change.

Alexander Jannaeus

יהונתן המלך

7.   AE prutah.
      O: Lily surrounded by Hebrew inscription (Yehonatan the king), border of dots.
      R: Upside down anchor within circle, surrounded by Greek inscription, ΒΑΣΙΛΕΩΣ ΑΛΕΞΑΝΔΡΟΥ (of Alexander the king). Mesh 5; AJC I, Group A.   150.00

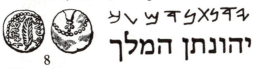

יהונתן המלך

8.   AE lepton.
      O: Upright palm branch surrounded by Hebrew inscription (Yehonatan the king), border of dots.
      R: Lily within border of dots. Mesh 6; AJC I, Group B. 2,250.00

9.   Pb (lead) 16mm.
    O: Anchor within circle surrounded by Greek inscription,
    ΒΑΣΙΛΕΩΣ ΑΛΕΞΑΝΔΡΟΥ.
    R: Traces of border of dots and obliterated Aramaic inscription
    (King Alexander). Mesh 7 and 7a; AJC, Group D.   100.00

10.   AE prutah.
    O: Anchor surrounded by Greek inscription, ΒΑΣΙΛΕΩΣ
    ΑΛΕΞΑΝΔΡΟΥ (of King Alexander).
    R: Star of eight rays surrounded by diadem, Hebrew inscription
    (Yehonatan the king) between rays. Mesh 8; AJC I, Group
    Ca.   40.00

11.   AE prutah.
    O: Anchor surrounded by Greek inscription, ΒΑΣΙΛΕΩΣ
    ΑΛΕΞΑΝΔΡΟΥ.
    R: Star with eight pellets instead of rays surrounded by diadem. No
    inscription between the pellets. BMC 87; AJC I, Group Cb.
                                                           45.00

*This coin appears in many varieties with various misstrikes, mistakes in
legends, and varieties in anchor and star types.*

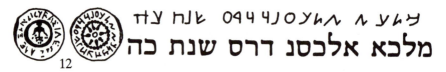

12.   AE lepton.
    O: Upside down anchor within circle surrounded by Greek inscrip-
    tion, ΒΑΣΙΛΕΩΣ ΑΛ'gEΞΑΝΔΡΟΥ. The letters LKE, made
    of dots often connected by fine lines, appear at the points of the
    anchor on some of the coins.
    R: Star of eight rays surrounded by border of dots and Aramaic
    inscription (King Alexander Year 25). Mesh 9 variety; with date
    AJC I, Group Cd.   35.00
                                           no date   25.00

The letters L KE, stylistically similar to lettering on Seleucid coins, signify the date, Year 25 of Jannaeus, corresponding to 78 B.C.E. *These coins often appear in crude varieties with illegible and incomplete inscriptions.*

13.   AE lepton.

        O: Upside down anchor within circle, barbaric or incomplete inscription.

        R: Star surrounded by border of dots, perhaps a barbaric inscription. Mesh 10 variety; AJC I, Group Ce.   20.00

This coin is found in innumerable varieties, some of which seem to carry crude linear designs instead of stars on reverse.

14.   AE prutah.

        O: Hebrew inscription (Yehonatan the high priest and the council of the Jews) surrounded by wreath.

        R: Double cornucopia adorned with ribbons and pomegranate arising between horns. Mesh 12; AJC I, Groupe E.   40.00

15.   AE prutah.

        O: Hebrew inscription (Yehonatan the high priest and the council of the Jews) surrounded by wreath.

        R: Double cornucopia adorned with ribbons and pomegranate arising between hours. Mesh 13 variety; AJC I, Group F.   40.00

16.   AE prutah.

        O: Hebrew inscription (Yehonatan the high priest and the council of the Jews) of the cursive style script (according to A. Kindler) surrounded by wreath.

        R: Double cornucopia adorned with ribbons and pomegranate arising between horns. Mesh 14 variety; AJC I, Group G.   45.00

17. AE prutah.
     O: Hebrew inscription (Yonatan the high priest and the council of
        the Jews) surrounded by wreath. Greek letters ΛΕΞΑ and parts
        of anchor/circle design remain from coin that has been over-
        struck (no. 7).
     R: Double cornucopia adorned with ribbons and pomegranate aris-
        ing between horns. Part of lily and Hebrew inscription remain
        from earlier coin. Mesh 17 and 17a; AJC I, Group I.   65.00
*It is interesting to note that the new design eliminates the designation "king"
in both Hebrew and Greek, and replaces it with the title "high priest".
Further, the ruler has modified the Hebrew spelling of his name from "Yehonatan" to "Yonatan", thus breaking up the combination of Hebrew letters
(YEHO-) used commonly as an abbreviation of the Lord's name. It is
possible that the bellicose, Hellenized Jannaeus made these changes as
concessions toward the rival Pharisees near the end of his life in an effort
to reconciliate his people.*

*Since there are such a tremendous number of these overstrikes it may be
assumed that most such coins were restruck before they ever left the mint
rather than upon recall from circulation.*

18. AE prutah.
     O: Crude Hebrew inscription (Yonatan the high priest and the coun-
        cil of the Jews) surrounded by wreath. Many letters are illegible.
     R: Double cornucopia adorned with ribbons and pomegranate aris-
        ing between horns. Mesh 15 variety; AJC I, Group H.   40.00
*Such coins appear in many varieties, the crude and incomplete inscrip-
tions, often with mistakes, being their hallmark. Note the new spelling of
the king's name as on the previous coin.*

19. AE prutah.
     O: Complete imitation of Hebrew inscription surrounded by highly
        stylized wreath. Inscription is totally illegible.
     R: Tiny schematic double cornucopia with pomegranate arising be-
        tween horns. Mesh 16 variety; AJC I, Group Hd.   40.00

John Hyrcanus II (Yehohanan), 67 and 63 to 40 B.C.E.
Judah Aristobulus II (Yehudah), 67 to 63 B.C.E.

Now Hyrcanus was heir to the kingdom, and to him did his mother commit it before she died; but Aristobulus was superior to him in power and magnanimity. (Josephus, *Wars*, I, VI:1)

After the death of Alexander Jannaeus, rule of the Land of Israel was inherited by his queen, Salome Alexandra (Shelomziyyon). She apparently issued no coins bearing her name. During her reign, Hyrcanus II, her oldest son, was appointed high priest and thus was regarded as heir to the throne.

Since Hyrcanus was weak, however, and not as politically sophisticated as his younger brother Aristobulus II, he became involved in a bitter struggle when his mother died. Aristobulus was apparently just the opposite of his brother and had inherited his father's bellicosity. At a skirmish between the two near Jericho, most of Hyrcanus's men went over to Aristobulus.

With Aristobulus now king and high priest, Hyrcanus received an honorary title, but no power, which he dearly wanted. His ambitions were encouraged by his advisor Antipater, an Arab from Idumaea who had been forcibly converted to Judaism 50 years earlier. Antipater was a rich chieftain and had already a good deal of power on his own. But he wanted more. He thought he might get it through the weak Hyrcanus, so he started to agitate for him to fight his younger brother and seize again the power Antipater said was rightfully his.

Hyrcanus, under Antipater's advice, fled Jerusalem to the Nabatean king Aretas III. By making territorial concessions to the Nabatean ruler, Hyrcanus induced him to join forces against Aristobulus. Their armies besieged Aristobulus in Jerusalem in 65 B.C.E.

At about this time Pompey's armies, led by the general Marcus Scaurus, marched into the East. Initially, Scaurus favored Aristobulus (probably due to bribes), but when Pompey arrived in Syria in 63 B.C.E. the two brothers laid their claims before him. Antipater went along to support Hyrcanus.

Pompey, feeling that Hyrcanus was the weaker of the brothers and hence less likely to cause trouble later, ruled that he was the rightful king. At this, Aristobulus and his followers fled to Jerusalem where they fortified themselves. But the great Pompey, terror of pirates and kings, followed. Aristobulus foolishly tricked and teased Pompey, pretending that he was going to surrender, but fleeing to temporary safety in Jerusalem instead. When Pompey's men burst into the city after a three-month siege they inflicted heavy casualties on the Jews. Pompey himself entered the Temple's Holy of Holies, the inner sanctuary, thus defiling it. For all practical purposes this act ended the great Hasmonean dynasty, for it would never recover even a fraction of its previous strength.

Aristobulus was captured and sent with his children to Rome, where he was ridiculed and paraded through the streets. (Later he would escape and again try, unsuccessfully, to regain control of Judaea.)

Now, as ruler, Hyrcanus II, all but totally subservient to Rome, was reappointed high priest. In 47 B.C.E. he was named "ethnarch," which meant "ruler of the people," but was clearly something less than king. (For numismatic evidence in this regard see coins 26–29.)

With the weak Hyrcanus ruling Judaea, Pompey easily cut its size by granting autonomy to several cities, including Gaza and Gadara. Furthermore, Pompey's general Gabinius was left as the governor of Syria, also charged with looking after Judaea. He divided the Land of Israel into five districts, mainly for taxation purposes.

Throughout the remainder of Hyrcanus II's rule, Antipater, closely allied with Rome, played a major—perhaps even the major—role in governing. This is best shown by the eventual succession of Antipater's son Herod to the throne. Furthermore, a number of Hyrcanus's coins carry monograms of the Greek letters A and Π, sometimes combined, which probably stand for Antipater himself.

The coins of Aristobulus II are relatively scarce, while those of Hyrcanus II are far more common. With the exception of the Greek monograms on the coins of Hyrcanus II, all the inscriptions on the coins of these brothers are in ancient Hebrew, and again many mistakes and abbreviated inscriptions occur. Designs on these coins include the cornucopia, plants, and palms, with a single coin depicting a helmet.

John Hyrcanus II

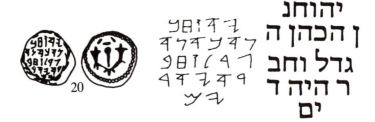

20.   AE prutah.
    O: Hebrew inscription (Yehohanan the high priest and the council of the Jews) surrounded by wreath.
    R: Double cornucopia adorned with ribbons and pomegranate arising between horns. Mesh 18; AJC I, Group K.   40.00

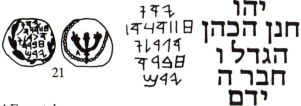

21. AE prutah.
O: Hebrew inscription (Yehohanan the high priest and the council of the Jews) surrounded by wreath.
R: Double cornucopia adorned with ribbons and pomegranate arising between horns. Tiny monogram A to lower left. Mesh 18a variety; AJC I, Group P.   40.00

22. AE prutah.
O: Hebrew inscription (Yehohanan the high priest and the council of the Jews) surrounded by wreath; Greek letter "A" above inscription.
R: Double cornucopia adorned with ribbons and pomegranate arising between horns, border of dots. Mesh 19; AJC I, Group M.   50.00

23. AE prutah.
O: Hebrew inscription (Yehohanan the high priest and the council of the Jews) surrounded by wreath.
R: Double cornucopia adorned with ribbons and pomegranate arising between horns; monogram (A Π?) below left. Mesh 20A variety; AJC I, Group N.   50.00

A number of interesting monogram varieties appear on these coins.

23a. AE prutah.
O: Hebrew inscription (as on coin no. 23, but different arrangement and style of letters) surrounded by wreath.
R: Same as coin no. 23 but *without* any monogram.   40.00

יהוחנן
הכהן הגר
ל וחבר ה
יהד ם

24. AE prutah.
O: Hebrew inscription (Yehohanan the high priest and the council of the Jews) surrounded by wreath.
R: Double cornucopia adorned with ribbons and pomegranate arising between horns; monogram "A" below left. Mesh 20A variety; AJC I, Group N.   50.00

יהוחנן
הכהן הג
דל ו חברה
יהדים

25. AE lepton.
O: Palm branch upright flanked by four lines of Hebrew inscription (Yehohanan the high priest and council of the Jews).
R: Lily; monogram "A" at left below flower. Mesh 21a; AJC I, Group O.   650.00

This coin is sometimes seen without monogram.

יהו
חנן הכה
ן הג דל ר
אש החב
ר הי

26. AE prutah.
O: Hebrew inscription (Yehohanan the high priest and head of the council of the Jews) surrounded by wreath.
R: Double cornucopia adorned with ribbons and pomegranate arising between horns; monogram ∴ below left. Mesh 22 variety; AJC I, Group S.   50.00

Meshorer notes that the addition of the designation "head" in the inscription is highly significant and is probably related to the designation "ethnarch" given by Julius Caesar to Hyrcanus II in 47 B.C.E.

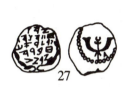

יהו
חנן הכהן
גדל ראש
חבר ה
י דים

27.   AE prutah.
      O: Hebrew inscription (Yehohanan the high priest and head of the
      council of the Jews) surrounded by wreath.
      R: Double cornucopia adorned with ribbons and pomegranate aris-
      ing between horns; monogram A below right. Mesh 23 variety;
      AJC I, Group S.   50.00
28.   AE lepton.
      O: Palm branch upright flanked by Hebrew inscription (Yehohanan
      the high priest and head of the community of the Jews) in four
      lines.
      R: Lily. Mesh 24; AJC I, Group T.   750.00

יהוחנן ה כהן הגדל
ראש   החבר הים

29.   AE double prutah.
      O: Double cornucopia with horns facing in same direction, adorned
      with ribbons, surrounded by Hebrew inscription (Yehohanan
      the high priest and head of the council of the Jews).
      R: Helmet with decorative crest facing right, border of dots. Mesh
      25; ACJ I, Group R.   6500.00

30.   AE prutah.
      O: Hebrew inscription (Yehohanan the high priest and head of the
      council of the Jews) surrounded by wreath.
      R: Double cornucopia with ribbons and pomegranate arising be-
      tween horns. Mesh 26 variety; AJC I, Group L.   50.00
*Kindler and Kanael consider that this coin, with its incomplete inscription
and primitive, block-style lettering, was issued under John Hyrcanus I. For
the best arguments clarifying both sides of this issue see Meshorer's Jewish
Coins of the Second Temple Period.*

31.   AE prutah.
       O: Hebrew inscription (Yehohanan the high priest . . .) surrounded
          by wreath.
       R: Double cornucopia adorned with ribbons and pomegranate aris-
          ing between horns. Mesh 27 variety; AJC I, Group Q.   40.00
*Kindler and Kanael also consider this coin, with its primitive inscription
and many mistakes, to have been issued under Hyrcanus I.*

Judah Aristobulus II

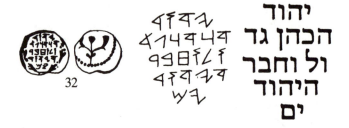

32.   AE prutah.
       O: Hebrew inscription (Yehudah the high priest and council of the
          Jews) surrounded by wreath.
       R: Double cornucopia adorned with ribbons and pomegranate aris-
          ing between horns. Mesh 28; AJC I, Group Ja.   150.00

33.   AE prutah.
       O: Hebrew inscription (of the same type, but in a different style
          from above) surrounded by wreath.
       R: Double cornucopia adorned with ribbons and pomegranate aris-
          ing between horns. Mesh 29; AJC I, Group Jb–Jc.   200.00

Mattathias Antigonus (Mattatayah), 40 to 37 B.C.E.

Out of hatred to Herod it was that he assisted Antigonus, the son of Aristobulus. (Josephus, *Wars*, I, XII:2)

By 40 B.C.E. Judaea was almost completely dominated by Rome. Antipater the Idumaean had been the power behind Hyrcanus II for some time, and his sons Phasael and Herod were the governors of Jerusalem and Galilee, respectively. Herod, all the while, had been gaining considerable power through political alliances, especially with Rome.

In the year 40, Mattathias Antigonus, youngest son of Aristobulus II and four generations removed from Judah Maccabee, bribed the Parthians (Rome's greatest foe in the area) under Orodes II to invade Jerusalem and help him win the crown and position of high priest, still held by his uncle, Hyrcanus II. (It is said that the bribe to Orodes included some 500 Jewish women.)

When the Parthians and men of Antigonus marched into Jerusalem, Hyrcanus II and Herod and his men retreated to the royal palace, while Antigonus and his forces occupied the Temple Mount. Herod escaped Jerusalem and eventually made his way to Rome, where he was officially designated king of Judaea in 40 B.C.E.

In his book *Judaea Weeping,* George Brauer relates this tale of Antigonus and his uncle Hyrcanus II: "Hyrcanus was not dangerous enough to kill, but Antigonus wanted his uncle's high-priestly office as well as the throne. It was said that when Hyrcanus was brought before him as a suppliant, Antigonus gnawed off the old man's ears. A high priest had to be without bodily blemish. Hyrcanus would never be high priest again."

Other historians note, however, that while this makes a nice story it is probably not true, and the chances are better that Hyrcanus was mutilated by the Parthians.

When Herod returned to Judaea to resume hostilities against Antigonus, he did not receive any substantial support from Ventidius, Antony's legate and eventual victor in the Parthian War. Herod battled Antigonus's forces for two more years until, after a siege of several months, Herod, with the Roman forces of C. Sossius, took Jerusalem and captured and killed Antigonus.

The coins of Antigonus are of poor quality. They have a high lead content, probably as a result of the demands of the constant wartime activities. Perhaps because of their poor substance, most of Antigonus's coins are minted on double-thick flans, an exception being the famous, and very rare, prutah showing the seven-branched menorah.

Since there was a prohibition of reproducing items used in the Temple ceremonies, many questions exist as to why Antigonus chose the menorah for one of his symbols. Some believe it was sacrilege. Meshorer wisely suggests, however, that Antigonus, faced with an increasingly powerful foe in Herod, issued the coin with the menorah as a "proclamation," to warn the Jews that it was forbidden to allow the Temple, and indeed the land, to fall into the hands of strangers. "It is our contention," Meshorer writes, "that this coin had no economic or financial but a propaganda value only, and therefore Antigonus had no scruples about reducing its weight, in contrast to the other [coins] which he struck on flans cast in closed molds." Thus it seems that this coin of Antigonus may have been a kind of a "last fling," fully expressing the spirit of the Maccabees, even in the great dynasty's dying days.

The coins of Antigonus have legends in both Greek and ancient Hebrew and are usually poorly preserved. They carry designs of the cornucopiae, barley ear, wreaths, the menorah, and the showbread table.

Mattathias Antigonus (Mattatayah)

34

מתתיה הכהן ה גדלח

34.   AE 22–23mm.
O: Double cornucopia with Hebrew inscription (Mattatayah the high priest and council of the Jews) around and between horns.
R: Ivy wreath tied at top with ribbons hanging down, surrounded by Greek inscription, ΒΑCΙΛΕΩC ΑΝΤΙΓΟΝΥ (of King Antigonus. Mesh 30; AJC I, Group U.   250.00
The inscription appears in many lettering variations.

35

מתתיה הכהן
הגדל ח

35.　AE 19.5mm.
　　O: Single cornucopia tied with ribbons, Hebrew inscription (Mat-
　　tatayah the high priest) around; sometimes vine leaf and grapes
　　hang from cornucopia.
　　R: Greek inscription (in 2, 3 or more lines) within wreath and border
　　of dots, BACIΛEOC/ ANTIΓONY. Mesh 31; AJC I, Group
　　V.　　　　　　　　　　　　　　　　　　　　　　　　　150.00
The inscriptions may also appear in many variations.

36.　AE 13–15mm.
　　O: Double cornucopia adorned with ribbons and *ear of barley* aris-
　　ing between horns, border of dots.
　　R: Hebrew inscription in retrograde (Mattatayah) surrounded by
　　wreath and border of dots. Mesh 33; AJC I, Group Y.　100.00

37.　AE 13mm.
　　O: Hebrew inscription (Mattatayah the high priest) surrounded by
　　wreath.
　　R: Double cornucopia adorned with ribbons and pomegranate aris-
　　ing between horns. Mesh 34; AJC I, Group W.　　　400.00

38.　AE 15mm.
　　O: Seven-branched menorah surrounded by Greek inscription
　　 BAΣIΛEΩΣ ANTIΓONOY.
　　R: Showbread table with traces of Hebrew inscription around. Mesh
　　36; AJC I, Group Z.　　　　　　　　　　　　　　9,000.00
This is the only ancient Jewish coin with the seven-branched menorah.
Meshorer speculates that this coin was issued mainly for its propaganda
value in the dying days of the reign of the last of the Hasmonean rulers.

Hasmonean Family Genealogical Table

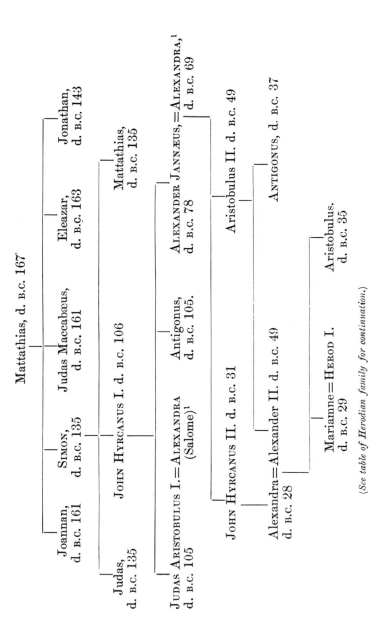

(See table of Herodian family for continuation.)

Herodian Family Genealogical Table

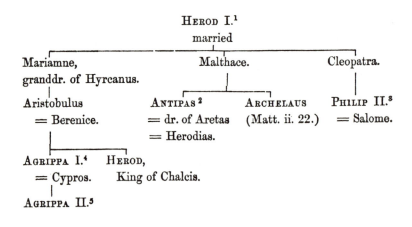

Herod I.[1]
married

Mariamne,
granddr. of Hyrcanus.

Aristobulus
= Berenice.

Agrippa I.[4]
= Cypros.

Agrippa II.[5]

Herod,
King of Chalcis.

Malthace.

Antipas[2]
= dr. of Aretas
= Herodias.

Archelaus
(Matt. ii. 22.)

Cleopatra.

Philip II.[3]
= Salome.

---

[1] Herod the King (Matt. ii. 1; Luke i. 5).

[2] Herod the Tetrarch (Matt. xiv. 1, 3; Luke iii. 1, 19; ix. 7); the King (Matt. xiv. 9); King Herod (Mark vi. 14).

[3] Philip [II.] the Tetrarch (Luke iii. 1).

[4] Herod the King (Acts xii.).

[5] King Agrippa (Acts xxv. 13; xxvi. 2 *seq.*).

5. HERODIAN COINS

Herod I (the Great), 40 B.C.E. to 4 C.E.

Now when Jesus was born in Bethlehem of Judea in the days of Herod the king . . . (Matthew 2:1. See also Matthew 2:1–13 and 16–18)

Herod was made king in 40 B.C.E. by a declaration of the Roman senate and the approval of Octavian (Augustus). In reality, however, Mattathias Antigonus was ruler of Judaea at the time and remained so for more than two years.

In 37 B.C.E., with help from the Roman general C. Sossius, Herod finally was able to besiege Jerusalem and capture it, along with Antigonus and his backers.

One of Herod's first official acts as king was to order death for 45 members of the Sanhedrin who had supported the Hasmoneans. This effectively reduced the power of the Sanhedrin to little more than that of a religious court.

Herod ruled Judaea completely at the grace of Rome. His administration was mainly Hellenistic in character and, indeed, one of Herod's continued policy goals seemed to be to strengthen the foreign element in Israel and to bring the kingdom completely into line as a strong link in the Roman Empire.

The Romans had actually resurrected the title "King of Judaea" for Herod, since he was not of priestly family and therefore could not occupy the office of high priest, yet had to be given a title equal or better in prestige. Furthermore, Antigonus had styled himself "king" on his coins and nothing less would do for Herod.

Herod realized that being from a non-priestly family meant potential problems with the Jewish people; so, to strengthen his ties with the royal Hasmonean family, he married Mariamne, a granddaughter of Hycanus II. Unfortunately for his family, however, Herod was paranoid about threats to his power.

When he took over the throne, therefore, he ignored the legal heir to the office of high priest even though he was Aristobulus III, his wife's brother. Instead he appointed Hananel, whom he brought back to Jerusalem from the Egyptian diaspora. This act caused Herod's mother-in-law to complain to Cleopatra, Queen of Egypt, whose Roman ties enabled her to wield power over Herod. Cleopatra compelled Herod to dismiss Hananel and appoint Aristobulus. But the young Hasmonean's popularity with the people grew and Herod decided to have him killed, a fate he also proclaimed for former king Hyrcanus II. These family murders caused severe tension between Herod and Mariamne, and in 29 B.C.E. Herod ordered his wife executed.

Not long after this Herod also sentenced his two sons by Mariamne, Antipater and Aristobulus, to death. It is said that when Augustus heard about the sentences he said, "It is better to be Herod's pig than his son." Still, the sentence stood and the sons were executed, thus eliminating every member of the Hasmonean family who might threaten Herod's throne in the immediate future.

Toward his policy of Hellenizing the region, Herod embarked on many construction and cultural projects. He built a seaport on the Mediterranean with palaces, temples, amphitheatres, and aqueducts of gleaming white limestone. He named the city Caesarea after Augustus, and it became the country's largest port. He also built the city of Sebaste on the site of Samaria.

Herod's pathologic suspicion caused him also to build a string of mountain fortresses leading toward Nabataea, which doubled as palatial resort homes for himself and his entourage. These fortresses were to serve Herod if he had to make a hasty retreat in case of insurrection. The sites included Herodium in Judaea, Herodion in Transjordan, and Massada on the Dead Sea.

Herod hoped he could partially mollify the Jews' feelings toward him by restoring the Temple. (Herod himself was a Jew, his father having been forcibly converted as a child when the lands in which he lived were conquered by the Hasmoneans.) He did it in a magnificent way: it took 10,000 commoners and 1,000 priests at least nine years to complete the project. They erected magnificent new walls of majestic stones—many of which can still be seen in Jerusalem today—doubled the Temple's size, and encircled it with beautiful columns, gates, and courtyards. Herod also enlarged and strengthened the fortress adjoining the Temple Mount and renamed it Antonia, after Mark Anthony.

Herod did not offend the Jews by bringing statues or other physical effigies into Jerusalem until late in his reign, when he affixed a golden eagle to the Temple gate.

With all of his building expenses and the other costs of a lavish court, such as gifts and bribes to relatives and Roman allies and heavy taxes to Rome, Herod amassed considerable debts. To pay them he taxed his people heavily. Josephus reports that "since he was involved in expenses greater than his means, he was compelled to be harsh to his subjects . . . since he was unable to mend his evil ways without harming his revenues, he exploited the ill will of the people to enrich himself privately."

In anticipation of his death, Herod ordered that at the time of his demise the leading Jews of Jerusalem were to be murdered: thus there would be no lack of mourners at his funeral. This final act, more than any other, depicts the relationship between Herod and his fellow Jews.

The great offense of which Herod has been accused through the ages is the "slaughter of the innocents," in which he allegedly ordered the killing of all the male babies in the area of Bethlehem because he heard that a future "king of the Jews" (Jesus) had been born. However, there is a great deal of scholarly disagreement with this account. Historian Michael Grant offers the current view in his book *Jesus: An Historian's Review of the Gospels*:

"About the date of Jesus' birth there are . . . perplexing problems. The belief that he was born in A.D. 1 only came into existence in the 6th century A.D. when a monk from South Russia living in Italy, Dionysius Exiguus, made a mathematical miscalculation. His birthdate should be reassigned to 6 or 5 or 4 B.C., though some prefer 11 or 7.

"Matthew's story of the Massacre of the Innocents by Herod the Great, because he was afraid of a child born at Bethlehem 'to be King of the Jews,' is a myth allegedly fulfilling a prophecy by Jeremiah and mirroring history's judgment of the great but evil potentate Herod, arising from many savage acts during the last years before his death in 4 B.C."

There has been considerable discussion over the monogram ₱ which appears on many of the early coins of Herod. B. Kanael has noted that it probably represents a combination of the Greek letters T P—a contraction for *trito*, or "third year". Says Kanael, "It is likely that Herod wanted to accentuate the fact that 37 B.C.E., which was in fact his first year as king, should be regarded as his third year, reckoned from 40 B.C.E. when Rome had appointed him". Meshorer counters that Herod's third year is more probably 40 B.C.E., counted from the year 42 B.C.E., when Herod was appointed tetrarch by Marc Antony.

In spite of his continuing adversary relationship with his own people, Herod (named "the Great" by writers foreign to his own land) minted coins with no symbols offensive to the Jews and no graven images, save a single bronze coin (no. 56) that shows the eagle Herod had affixed to the Temple gate. Herod was the first Jewish ruler to use exclusively Greek inscriptions on his coins.

Herod I

39. AE 8 prutot.
   O: Tripod with ceremonial bowl (lebes) above, date (LΓ—Year 3, 40 B.C.E.) and monogram ₱ in field left and right, surrounded by Greek inscription, ΒΑΣΙΛΕΩΣ ΗΡΩΔΟΥ (of King Herod).
   R: Thymiaterion (a kind of incense burner), star above, flanked by two palm branches. AJC II, 235, 1.   400.00

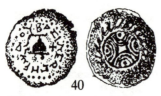 

40. AE 4 prutot.
O: Crested helmet flanked by date and monogram (as above) in field left and right, surrounded by Greek inscription, ΒΑΣΙΛΕΩΣ ΗΡΩΔΟΥ.
R: Shield with decorated rim. AJC II, 235, 2. 450.00

41. AE 2 prutot.
O: Winged caduceus flanked by date and monogram (as above) in field left and right, surrounded by Greek inscription, ΒΑΣΙΛΕΩΣ ΗΡΩΔΟΥ.
R: Pomegranate on branch. AJC II, 235, 3. 650.00

42. AE prutah.
O: Aphlaston flanked by date and monogram in field left and right (as above), surrounded by Greek inscription, ΒΑΣΙΛΕΩΣ ΗΡΩΔΟΥ.
R: Palm branch with objects (leaves?) on either side. AJC II, 235, 5. 500.00

43. AE 2 prutot.
O: Cross surrounded by closed diadem, surrounded by Greek inscription, ΒΑΣΙΛΕΩΣ ΗΡΩΔΟΥ.
R: Tripod table flanked by palm branches. AJC II, 236, 7. 125.00
The diadem is sometimes open.

44. AE prutah.
O: Cross surrounded by closed diadem, surrounded by Greek inscription, mostly illegible, ΒΑΣΙΛΕΩΣ ΗΡΩΔΟΥ.
R: Tripod table. AJC II, 236, 10. 85.00

45. AE prutah.
O: Greek inscription scattered in field, ΒΑΣΙΛΕΩΣ ΗΡΩΔΟΥ.
R: Tripod table within circle of dots. AJC II, 236, 11. 85.00

46.　AE prutah.
　　O: Similar to no. 45, open diadem.
　　R: Tripod table within circle of dots. AJC II, 236, 12.　　85.00
47.　AE prutah.
　　O: Similar to no. 46.
　　R: Tiny tripod table.　BA . . . . OY.　AJC II, 236, 13.　　95.00

48

49

48.　AE lepton.
　　O: Tiny tripod surrounded by Greek inscription,　BACIΛEΩC
　　HPΩΔOY.
　　R: Two crossed palm branches. AJC II, 237, 14.　　150.00
49.　AE lepton.
　　O: Tiny tripod surrounded by Greek inscription,　BACIΛEΩC
　　HPΩΔOY.
　　R: Palm branch upright within circle. AJC II, 237, 15.　　150.00
50.　AE prutah.
　　O: Greek inscription around tripod table,　HPΩΔOY　BA-
　　CIΛEΩC.
　　R: Palm branch upright. AJC II, 237, 15.　　350.00

51

52

53

51.　AE prutah.
　　O: Greek inscription within border of dots,　BACIΛEYC
　　HPΩΔHC.
　　R: Anchor within wreath. AJC II, 237, 18.　　150.00
52.　AE prutah.
　　O: Greek inscription in circles surrounded by dots,　BACIΛEΩC
　　HPΩΔOY.
　　R: Anchor surrounded by a circle decorated with Y-like design.
　　AJC II, 238, 19.　　50.00
53.　AE prutah.
　　O: Greek inscription surrounded by a circle of dots,　BACIΛEΩC
　　HPΩΔOY.
　　R: Anchor surrounded by circle decorated with vertical or V-like
　　lines. AJC II, 238, 20.　　50.00

54.   AE prutah.
      O: Anchor surrounded by Greek inscription, HPWΔ BACI.
      R: Double cornucopia with caduceus rising between, dots above.
      AJC II, 237, 17.   40.00
55.   AE prutah.
      O: Anchor surrounded by Greek inscription, partially retrograde,
      IƆAB HPW.
      R: Double cornucopia with caduceus rising between, dots above.
      AJC II, 237, 17k.   75.00
The Greek inscription on this coin appears in many varieties.

56.   AE lepton.
      O: Cornucopia with Greek inscription above and below, BACIΛ
      HPWΔ.
      R: Eagle standing right. AJC II, 238, 23.   65.00
*This is apparently the first coin issued by a Jewish ruler for use by Jews
with a graven image upon it. The eagle is said to represent the golden bird
Herod placed above the Temple entrance.*

57.   AE lepton.
      O: Anchor surrounded by Greek inscription, BACIΛEΩC HP-
      WΔOY.
      R: War galley surrounded by dots. AJC II, 238, 22.   150.00

Herod Archelaus, 4 B.C.E. to 6 C.E.

*But when he heard that Archelaus did reign in Judea in the room of his
father Herod, he was afraid to go thither . . .   (Matthew 2:22)*

Archelaus was the oldest son of Herod by his Samaritan wife Malthrace.
In Herod's final will he designated Archelaus the future king of Judaea
and Samaria. But since Herod's title was not itself hereditary, the suggested
heir needed confirmation by Rome. After the mourning period for his
father, Archelaus prepared to voyage there.
    Before he left, however, he met with a number of spokesmen for various
groups in the Temple area. A crowd gathered and began to test the king-

designate's sincerity and good will by making considerable demands. They wanted him, for example, to drastically reduce taxes. Members of the crowd also began to bewail a group of scholars who had been executed by Herod for cutting the golden eagle down from the Temple gates. These activities led to riots against Archelaus's men, which were intensified by the huge influx of people into Jerusalem because of the Passover festival. Archelaus soon lost his patience and sent his soldiers against the crowd, killing some 3,000 Jews, according to Josephus.

When Archelaus arrived in Rome, others, who came from Judaea, petitioned the Emperor Augustus to end the rule of the Herodian family and annex Judaea to the Roman Province of Syria. Herod's second son, Antipas, also petitioned Augustus for a royal position.

Augustus said he believed that Archelaus deserved the kingship, but he altered the terms of Herod's will, abolishing the Judaean monarchy and naming Archelaus "ethnarch" over Judaea, Samaria, and Idumaea. The emperor promised that the title "king" would also be forthcoming if Archelaus governed well.

As Josephus notes, however, once he was "established as ethnarch Archelaus was unable to forget the old quarrels and treated not only Jews but even Samaritans so brutally that both peoples sent embassies to accuse him before Caesar, with the result that in the ninth year of his rule he was banished to Vienna in Gaul, and his property transferred to Caesar's treasury."

Archelaus's territories were now annexed to the province of Syria and placed under the direct rule of the Procurator Coponius.

The "Parable of the Pounds" (Luke 19:14) mentions a hated ruler, believed to have been Archelaus: "But his citizens hated him, and sent a message after him, saying, we will not have this man to reign over us."

The coins of Archelaus each carry the word "ethnarch" or its abbreviation in Greek. He did not use graven images or other symbols offensive to the Jews on his coins. Many of the symbols on his coins were drawn from those of his father, since Archelaus inherited his mint.

Archelaus

58.   AE prutah.
      O: Anchor surrounded by Greek inscription, HPWΔ (Herod).
      R: Double cornucopia adorned with ribbons and caduceus arising
         between horns, inscription EΘN to right, N above. AJC II,
         239, 1b.   80.00

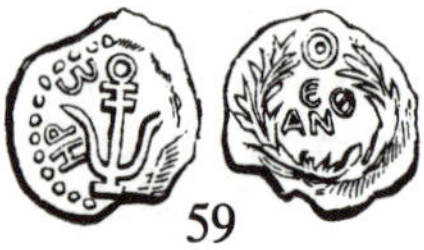

59

60

59. AE prutah.
   O: Anchor with long, slender arms surrounded by Greek inscription, HPWΔOY.
   R: Greek inscription ΕΘΑΝ (ethnarch), surrounded by wreath. AJC II, 239, 2b. 90.00

60. AE prutah.
   O: Prow of galley facing right, Greek inscription, HPW.
   R: Greek inscription ΕΘΝ surrounded by wreath, border of dots. AJC II, 240, 5. 50.00

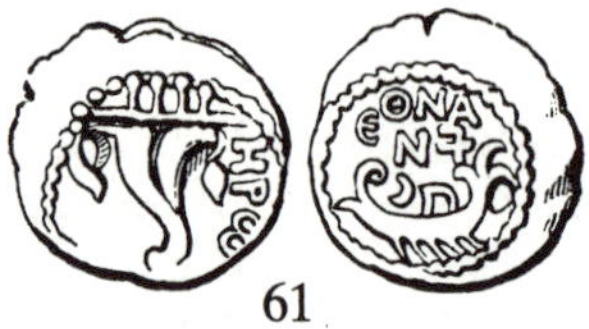

61

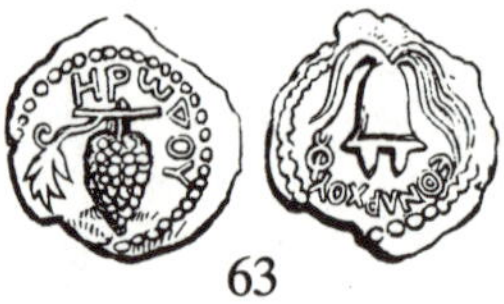

63

61. AE 2 prutot.
   O: Double cornucopia with both horns turned to the right, Greek inscription in field, HϤWΔOY.
   R: War galley facing left with aphlaston, oars, cabin, ram, Greek inscription above, ΕΘΝΑΡΧΗC (ethnarch). AJC II, 239, 3. 300.00

62. AE prutah.
   O: Double cornucopia with both horns turned to the right, Greek inscription in field, HPWΔ.
   R: War galley left with ram, oars and ophlaston, Greek inscription above, ΕΘΝ ϤΑ. AJC II, 240, 4. 150.00

This coin, as well as the previous one also occurs with the cornucopias turned to the left.

63. AE prutah.
   O: Bunch of grapes on vine with small leaf on left, Greek inscription begins above, HPWΔOY.
   R: Tall helmet with crest viewed from front, caduceus below left, inscription below, ΕΘΝΑΡΧΟΥ. AJC II, 241, 6. 50.00
   Varieties 75.00

This coin appears occasionally with the inscription reversed as to the side of the coin, as well as with errors in spelling and crude style. As usual with such varieties, they occasionally command premium prices, but they must be viewed as "mistakes" rather than new coin types.

Herod Antipas, 4 B.C.E. to 40 C.E.

The same day there came certain of the Pharisees, saying unto him, Get thee out, and depart hence; for Herod will kill thee. And he said unto them, Go ye, and tell that fox . . . (Luke 13:31,32)
And when the daughter of the said Herodias came in and danced, and pleased Herod . . . the kind said unto the damsel, ask me whatsoever thou wilt . . . And she came in . . . and asked saying, I will that thou give me by and by in a charger the head of John the Baptist. (Mark 6:22–25)

(Herod Antipas is also mentioned in the following verses: Matthew 14:1, 14:3, 14:6, 14:9; Mark 6:14–27; Luke 3:1, 3:19, 9:9, 23:7–15; Acts 5:27, 13:1.)

Antipas, son of Herod the Great, was full brother to Archelaus. They and their half-brother, Philip, had been educated in Rome. Herod willed Antipas the territories of Galilee and Perea, the Jewish portion of Transjordan.

Antipas's territory and title of "tetrarch" were confirmed by Augustus. His first capital was Sepphoris, but he moved it to Tiberias, the city he had built on the Sea of Galilee after Augustus died. The city was named for the new emperor to win his favor.

Called "that fox" by Jesus, Antipas is usually the "Herod" mentioned in the Bible. He ordered the execution of John the Baptist at the behest of his wife, Herodias, after her daughter by an earlier marriage, Salome, had pleased Antipas with a dance.

It was to Antipas that Pontius Pilate sent Jesus when he learned the man was a Galilean:

As soon as he knew that he belonged unto Herod's jurisdiction he sent him to Herod who himself was also in Jerusalem at the time. . . . Then he questioned with him in many words; but he answered him nothing. . . . And Herod with his men of war set him at nought, and mocked him, and arrayed him in a gorgeous robe, and sent him again to Pilate. (Luke 23:7–15)

When Caligula became emperor in 37 C.E., Agrippa I, grandson of Herod the Great, gained increased favor in Rome. He plotted to make his uncle Antipas appear to be a traitor to Rome and succeeded in this plot. He was no doubt aided by Antipas's unrestrained ambition and greed. Thus Caligula banished Antipas to Lugdunum in Gaul and confiscated his property, adding it to Agrippa's kingdom.

The coins of Antipas, all rare, are usually found in below average condition. They all carry a reed, palm branch, or palm tree, save one which depicts a bunch of dates, and inscriptions within wreaths. Except for the last year, all carry the name of the city in which they were struck, Tiberias. The Antipas coins of each known date were apparently struck in four denominations.

Herod Antipas

64. AE full denomination.
     O: Reed upright with date LKΔ   (Year 24) in field, surrounded
     by Greek inscription, HPWΔ   TETPAP   (of Herod the Te-
     trarch).
     R: Greek inscription, TIBE   PIAC   (Tiberias) surrounded by
     wreath, border dots. AJC II, 242, 1.   850.00

64   66

65. AE ¼ denomination.
     O: Reed upright with date LKΔ   (Year 24) in field, surrounded
     by Greek inscription, HPWΔOTETP (of Herod the Tetrarch).
     R: Greek inscription, TIB PIAC, surrounded by wreath, border
     dots. AJC II, 242, 3.   550.00

66. AE ½ denomination.
     O: Upright palm branch with date LΛΔ   (Year 34) in field, sur-
     rounded by Greek inscription, HPWΔOY TETPAPXOY.
     R: Greek inscription, TIBE PIAC, surrounded by wreath. AJC
     II, 242, 10.   750.00

*Similar coins also appear with the dates LΛΓ, LΛC, LΛZ, LMΓ. The
coins also occur in smaller denominations.*

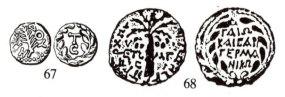

67   68

67. AE ⅛ denomination.
     O: Upright palm branch with date LΛΔ (Year 34) in field, sur-
     rounded by Greek inscription, HPWΔOY.
     R: Greek inscription TC, surrounded by wreath. AJC II, 242, 12.
                                                                   550.00

68. AE full denomination.
     O: Palm tree with two bunches of dates, date LMΓ (Year 43)
     and Greek inscription very hard to distinguish.
     R: Greek inscription ΓAIΩKAICAΓEPMANIKΩ (Gaius Caesar
     Germanicus—Caligula) surrounded by wreath. AJC II,
     243,17.   1,250.00

A primitive-style version of this coin also exists.

68a   69

68a.   AE full denomination.
        O: Upright palm branch with date LMΓ (Year 43) in field, sur-
        rounded by Greek inscription ΗΡΩΔΗC ΤΕΤΡΑΡΧΗC
        (Herod the Tetrarch).
        R: Greek inscription ΓΑΙΩ ΚΑΙCΑ ΡΙΓΕΡ ΜΑΝ (Gaius Cae-
        sar Germanicus—Caligula) within wreath. AJC II, 243,18.
                                                              850.00

69.   AE ¼ denomination.
        O: Small bunch of dates, hanging, date (LMΓ—Year 43) in field,
        Greek inscription around, ΗΡΩΔΗC ΤΕΤΡ . . .
        R: Greek inscription, ΓΑΙΩ ΚΑΙCΑ (Gaius Caesar) surrounded
        by wreath. AJC II, 243, 19.   1250.00

Herod Philip II, 4 B.C.E. to 34 C.E.

Now in the 15th year of the reign of Tiberius Caesar, Pontius Pilate being
governor of Judea and Herod being tetrarch of Galilee, and his brother
Philip tetrarch of Ituraea and of the reign of Trachonitas . . . (Luke 3:1)

(Herod Philip II is also mentioned in the following verses: Matthew 14:3;
Mark 6:17–29; Luke 3:19.)
    Son of Herod I and Cleopatra of Jerusalem, Philip was educated with
his older brothers, Archelaus and Antipas, in Rome. He received the final
portion of his father's kingdom—the northeastern section—as well as the
title "Tetrarch," like his brother Antipas.
    Philip founded the city of Caesarea Philippi, also called Paneas, which
he used as his capital:

When Jesus came into the coasts of Caesarea Philippi, he asked his disciples
. . . (Matthew 16:13)

Philip was apparently a peace-loving man and a good administrator.
Since few Jews lived in his territories, he apparently felt free to strike coins
with his own portrait: he was the first Jewish ruler to do so. He also placed
Roman imperial portraits on his coins, as well as a representation of the
Roman temple at Caesarea Philippi.

Philip was the first husband of the notorious Salome, his own niece. Upon his death, she married Aristobulus, king of Chalcis. Philip's land were then annexed to the Roman province of Syria, but in 37 C.E. they were given to Agrippa I. Philip was buried at Bethsaida, which he had renamed Julias in honor of Julia, daughter of Augustus.

Herod Philip II

70.   AE 24mm.
      O: Heads of Augustus and Livia facing right surrounded by Greek inscription ΣΕΒΑΣΤ . . . (Augustus).
      R: Tetrastyle temple with date between columns Θ (Year 9), inscription ΕΠΙ ΦΙΛΙΠΠΟΥ ΤΕΤΡΑΡ . . . (of Philip the Tetrarch). AJC II, 245, 6.   1350.00

70a. AE 24mm.
      O: Bareheaded head of Augustus to right, KAICAP CEBACTOY (Caesar Augustus).
      R: Bareheaded head of Philip to right, ΦΙΛΙΠΠΟΥ ΤΕΤΡΑΡΧΟΥ (of Philip the Tetrarch); date LE (Year 5 = 1–2 C.E.) in field. AJC II, 244, 1.   2,000.00

71.   AE 16mm.
      O: Head of Augustus right, surrounded by Greek inscription, CEBACTΩ KAICAP (Augustus Caesar).
      R: Tetrastyle temple with date between columns LIB (Year 12 = 8/9 C.E.), and Greek inscription around, ΦΙΛΙΠΠΟΥ ΤΕΤΡΑΡΧΟΥ. AJC II, 244, 3.   1,000.00

71a. AE 11mm.
      O: Bareheaded head of Philip to right, ΦΙΛΙΠΠΟΥ (of Philip).
      R: Date in wreath, LΛΔ (Year 34 = 30/31 C.E.). AJC II, 246, 12.   1,100.00

71b. AE 14mm.
      O: Draped bust of Livia, right, inscription around, ΙΟΥΛΙΑ CEBACTH (Julia the Queen).
      R: Hand holds three ears of corn, inscription around, ΚΑΡΠΟΦΟΡΟC (fruit bearing), LΛΔ (Year 34 = 30/31 C.E.). AJC II, 278, 1.   750.00

72. AE 17.5mm.
O: Head of Tiberius right, surrounded by Greek inscription
TIBEPIOC CEBACTOC KAICAP (Tiberius Augustus Cae-
sar).
R: Tetrastyle Temple with date between columns LΛZ (Year 37 =
33/34 C.E.) and Greek inscription around, ΦIΛIΠΠOY
TETPAPXOY. AJC II, 246, 14.   1,100.00

*Coins of Herod Phillip II listed above occur with variety of dates
occurring on the same types. Plate 72a shows a coin dated LIΘ
(Year 19).*

Agrippa I, 37 to 44 C.E.

> *Now about that time Herod [Agrippa] the king stretched forth his hands
> to vex certain of the church. And he killed James the brother of John with
> the sword.* (Acts 12:1–2)

(Agrippa I is the "Herod" who is mentioned throughout verses 1–23 of
the book of Acts.)

Grandson of Herod I and Mariamne the Hasmonean, Agrippa was educated in Rome, where he came to know both Gaius (Caligula) and Claudius. When the Emperor Tiberius heard that Agrippa had wished him dead
in order that his friend Gaius could become "lord of the world," he had
Agrippa imprisoned for such treasonous ideas.

Upon Tiberius's death, however, Caligula released Agrippa and made
him tetrarch over the former domain of Philip, his uncle. Two years later
Antipas, nagged on by his wife, also went to Caligula and asked for more
power. But Caligula became annoyed at this and instead banished Antipas
to Spain, naming Agrippa over his territories as well.

In 41, when Claudius became emperor, he bestowed upon Agrippa the
entire kingdom of his forebears. This made him the first and only true heir
to Herod the Great.

As the grandson of Mariamne the Hasmonean, thus a direct de-
scendant of the Maccabees as well, Agrippa was honored and respected
by the Jews. His initial unquestioning loyalty to Rome eventually gave way
to deep religious and nationalistic feelings, and Agrippa soon set about
surrounding Jerusalem "with fortifications so huge that had they been
finished they would have made it futile for the Romans to attempt a seige".
But before the wall was finished Agrippa I died in Caesarea in 44 C.E. at
age 54.

Agrippa, like Philip before him, struck his own portrait on his coins,
although these and others with graven images were meant to circulate
outside of areas with heavy Jewish population in his kingdom. Special coins
struck with symbols inoffensive to the Jews circulated in these areas (no.
75).

Agrippa I

73   74

73.   AE 20mm.
      O: Bust Agrippa I right; inscription around,   BACIΛEWC
      ΑΓΡΙΠΠΑ (of King Agrippa).
      R: Agrippa II rides horse to right; inscription around,   ΑΓΡΙΠΠΑ
      ΥΙΟΥ BACIΛEΩC, and date LB (Year 2). Struck 38/39 C.E.
      AJC II, 247,1.   2,500.00

74.   AE 23mm.
      O: Laureate bust Caligula left; inscription around,   ΓΑΙΩ ΚΑΙΣΑΡΙ
      ΣΕΒΑΣΤΩ (Gaius Caesar Augustus).
      R: Germanicus stands in quadriga to right; inscription,   ΝΟΜΙΣ
      ΒΑΣΙΛΕΩΣ ΑΓΡΙΠΠΑ, LE (coin of King Agrippa, Year 5).
      Struck 41 C.E. AJC II, 247, 2.   3,000.00

79.   AE 15mm.
      O: Bust of young Agrippa II left; inscription around, ΒΑΣΙΛΕΩΣ
      ΑΓΡΙΠΠΑ (King Agrippa).
      R: Double cornucopias, crossed at bases; inscription around, ΒΑΣ
      ΑΓΡΙΠΠΑ ΦΙΛΟ KAICAP (King Agrippa, friend of
      Caesar), date in field LE (Year 5 = 41/42 C.E.). AJC II, 247,
      4.   3,500.00
*With the discovery of a better specimen, Meshorer has corrected the at-
tribution of this coin to Agrippa I, thus this coin is numbered out of sequence.*

75

75.   AE prutah.
      O: Umbrella or canopy with fringes; inscription around,   BA-
      CIΛEWC ΑΓΡΙΠΑ.
      R: Three ears of barley growing between two leaves, flanked by
      date, LS (Year 6). Struck 42/43 C.E. AJC II, 249, 11.   50.00
This coin is frequently found with striking and/or engraving errors.

76   76a

76.   AE 25mm.
       O: Laureate bust Claudius right; inscription around, TIBEPIOC
          KAICAP CEBACTWC ΓEPM (Tiberius Caesar Augustus
          Germanicus).
       R: Distyle temple containing four figures in various standing and
          kneeling postures, possibly exchanging small objects, date LZ
          (Year 7) in center and inscription around, AΓPIΠΠAC
          ΦIΛOKAICAP BACIΛEYWC MEΓAC (Agrippa, friend of
          the great Caesar). Struck 43/44 C.E. AJC II, 249, 8.   5,000.00

76a.   AE 21mm.
       O: Agrippa I, left, and Herod of Chalcis, right, crown Emperor
          Claudius with a wreath while he sacrifices with patera over altar;
          inscription around BAΣ AΓPIΠΠAΣ ΣEB KAIΣAP BAΣ
          HPΩΔHΣ (The King Agrippa, the Augustus Caesar, the King
          Herod).
       R: Wreath enclosing two clasped hands, inscription in two concen-
          tric circles, OPKAI BAΣ ME AΓPIΠΠA ΠP ΣEB
          KAIΣAPA K ΣYNKΛHTON K ΔHMO PΩM ΦIΛI K
          ΣYNMAX AYTIY (A vow and treaty of friendship and alli-
          ance between the great King Agrippa and Augustus Caesar, the
          Senate and the people of Rome); at one o'clock on this specimen
          is an oval countermark of male head to left. AJC II, 248, 5a.
                                                               5,500

76b

76b.   AE 25mm.
       O: Diademed, draped bust of Agrippa I to right, inscription around,
          BACIΛEWC MEΓAC AΓPIΠΠAC ΦIΛOKAI (Agrippa the
          great friend of Caesar).
       R: Tyche stands left, her right hand on rudder and her left holding
          palm branch, surrounded by inscription, KAICAPIA H
          ΠPOΣ TΩ CEBACTΩ ΛIMHNI (Caesarea situated near
          the port of Sebastos); date LZ (Year 7 = 43 C.E.) in right field.
          AJC II, 248, 6.   5,000.00

Herod of Chalcis, 41 to 48 C.E.
Aristobulus of Chalcis, 57 to 92 C.E.

*Salute Apelles approved in Christ. Salute them which are of Aristobulus'
household.* (Romans 16:10)

The descendants of Herod I were extremely loyal to Rome, and thus were
given both rank and privilege.

Herod of Chalcis was the brother of Agrippa I. He was made king of
the Land of Chalcis in Lebanon at the foot of Mt. Hermon. He was one
of the three husbands of his niece Berenice, the same woman who was
Titus's lover and almost married him.

Herod of Chalcis was given the position of "guardian" of the Temple
and he was entitled to appoint the high priests, a duty which he exercised
three times.

Upon Herod III's death his nephew (and brother-in-law) Agrippa II
took over his kingdom. Later Agrippa gave up this throne and moved to
Philip's former kingdom.

Herod III's son, Aristobulus of Chalcis, struck coins with the portrait
of his wife Salome. This is the same Salome who had danced before Herod
Antipas and, at the urging of her mother, demanded the head of John the
Baptist.

Herod of Chalcis

77

77.   AE 23mm.
O: Bust of Herod of Chalcis to right; surrounded by inscription,
ΒΑΣΙΛΕΩΣ ΗΡΩΔΗC ΦΙΛΟΚΛΑΥΔΙΟC (King Herod,
friend of Claudius).

R: Within a wreath is inscription and date ΚΛΑΥΔΙΩ ΚΑΙΣΑ
ΡΙ ΣΕΒΑΣΤΩ ΕΤΓ (Claudius Caesar Augustus—Year 3).
Struck 43 C.E. AJC II, Supp. IV, 1.   4,000.00

Aristobulus of Chalcis

78.   AE 19mm.
O: Diademed bust of Aristobulus of Chalcis to left; surrounded by
inscription, ΕΤΙΗ ΒΑCΙΛΕΩC ΑΡΙCΤΟΒΟΥΛΟΥ (of King
Aristobulus).
R: Diademed bust of Salome to left; surrounded by inscription,
ΒΑCΙΛΙCCΗC ΣΑΛΩΜΗC (Queen Salome). AJC II, Supp.
IV, 5.   6,000.

Agrippa II, 56 to 95 c.e.

> *King Agrippa, believest thou the prophets? I know that thou believest.*
> *Then Agrippa said unto Paul, Almost thou persuadest me to be a Christian.*
> (Acts 26:27, 28)

(Agrippa II is involved in the action throughout Acts 25:13–27 and 26:1–32.)

When his father died in 44, the young Agrippa was only 17, so Claudius again brought the Jewish kingdom under direct rule of Rome, sending Procurator Cuspius Fadius and later the apostate Jew Tiberius Alexander to govern.

But when brother of Agrippa I, Herod, King of Chalcis, died, Claudius gave his throne to Agrippa II. Not long before he died, Claudius transferred Agrippa to a larger kingdom, giving him Philip's old tetrarchy as well as some other areas.

The next emperor, Nero, also added to Agrippa II's kingdom, giving him Abila and Julias in Peraea and Taricheae and Tiberias in Galilee. He then appointed the Procurator Antonius Felix as ruler of the rest of Judaea.

In addition to his northern lands Agrippa II was also given the right to oversee the affairs of the Temple at Jerusalem, and to appoint the High Priest. This made him a frequent visitor to the holy city, he was often accompanied by his sister Julia Berenice, with whom he may have had an incestuous relationship. Berenice was also a longtime lover of Titus.

Agrippa II and Berenice pleaded unsuccessfully with their people not to begin the war that became the First Revolt against Rome.

Agrippa II ruled for nearly 50 years, surviving the destruction of the Temple by some 25 years. His coins carry his own portrait as well as those of four of the eight emperors under whom he ruled: Nero, Vespasian, Titus, and Domitian.

Some of the coins of Agrippa II carry two dates (nos. 82 & 83). These apparently are based upon two separate dating eras of Agrippa II, one beginning in 56 C.E. and another beginning in 61 C.E., when Agrippa refounded the city of Paneas, renaming it Neronias in honor of Nero. Indeed, the two double-dated coins carry dates separated by a five-year period.

Agrippa II

Under Nero (era beginning 56 C.E.)

79. This coin is now attributed to Agrippa I and is listed before coin 75.

80   81

80. AE 18mm.
    O: Laureate head Nero right; inscription around, ΝΕΡΩΝ ΚΑΙ-
    ΣΑΡΣΕΒΑΣΤ . . . (Nero Caesar Augustus).
    R: Inscription in 5 lines, ΕΠΙ ΒΑΣΙΛΕ ΑΓΡΙΠΠ ΝΕΡΩΝΙ Ε
    (by King Agrippa, Nero), surrounded by circle, wreath, border
    of dots (E = Year 5). Struck 61 C.E. AJC II, 250, 2.   400.00
    This coin as well as two of the same type but different denominations were struck to commemorate Agrippa's refounding of Panias as Neronias. PLATE 80 shows the smallest denomination of the type.
81. AE 17mm.
    O: Bust of Agrippa II left; inscription around, ΒΑΣΙΛΕΩΣ
    ΑΓΡΙΠΠΟΥ.
    R: Anchor with date, LI (Year 10) in field. Struck 66 C.E. AJC II,
    250, 4.   3,000.00

82   83

82. AE 14/15mm.
    O: Bust of Tyche right; inscription around, ΝΕΡΩΝΙΑΔ ΚΑΙΣΑΡΙ
    ΑΓΡΙΠΠΑ (Caesar Neronias Agrippa).
    R: Double cornucopias crossed at base with winged caduceus arising between horns, inscription around, ΒΑΣ ΑΓΡ ΕΤΟΥΣ
    ΑΙ ΤΟΥ ΚΑΙ ϛ (Years 6 and 11 of King Agrippa). Struck
    67 C.E. AJC II, 250, 5.   3,000.00

83. AE 13mm.
   O: Hand right holding ears of barley and fruit; inscription around, ΒΑCΙΛΕΩC ΜΑΡΚΟΥ ΑΓΡΙΠΠΟΥ (King Marcus Agrippa).
   R: Monogram (Year 6) surrounded by inscription, ΕΤΟΥC ΑΙ ΤΟΥ⌐(Year 11), all within circle. Struck 67 C.E. AJC II, 250, 6.   3,000.00

Under Flavian Rule (era beginning 61 C.E.)

84

84. AE 18.2mm.
   O: Laureate bust Vespasian right, inscription around, ΑVΤΟΚΡΑ ΟVΕCΠΑCΙ ΚΑΙCΑΡΙ CΕΒΑCΤΩ (Emperor Vespasian Caesar Augustus).
   R: Tyche standing left on platform holding full cornucopia in left hand and ears of corn in right, star in field top left; inscription and date across field, ΕΤΟΥ ΚΖΒΑ ΑΓΡΙΠΠΑ (Year 27 of King Agrippa). Struck 83 C.E. AJC II, 256, 38.   600.00
This coin is found with a variety of dates.

85

85. AE 27mm.
   O: Laureate bust Titus right, inscription around, ΑΥΤΟ ΚΡΑΤΙΤΟC ΚΑΙCΑΡ CΕΒΑC (Emperor Titus Caesar Augustus).
   R: Tyche standing left on platform holding full cornucopia in left hand and ears of barley in right; inscription and date across field, ΕΤΟΥ ΙΘΒΑ ΑΓΡΙΠΠΑ (Year 19 of King Agrippa). Struck 75 C.E. AJC II, 256, 17.   750.00
This coin is found with a variety of dates.

86.   AE 23/25mm.
       O: Laureate bust Titus right, inscription around, AVTOKP TITOC
       KAICAP CEBACTOC.
       R: Nike advances to right holding wreath in right hand and palm
       branch over shoulder in left; in field, star, inscription and date,
       ETO KSBA ΑΓΡΙΠΠΑ (Year 26 of King Agrippa). Struck
       82 C.E. AJC II, 255, 32a.   500.00
87.   AE 23mm.
       O: Laureate bust Domitian right; inscription around, ΔΟΜΙΤΙΑ
       KAICAP (Caesar Domitian).
       R: Nike stands left writing on shield resting on her right knee;
       inscription and date across field, LIΔ BACI ΑΓΡΙΠΟΥ (Year
       14 of King Agrippa). Struck 70 C.E. AJC II, 251, 11.   300.00

88.   AE 14.5mm.
       O: Bust of Domitian right, inscription around, ΔΟΜΙΤΙΑΝΟC
       KAICAP.
       R: War galley with three-lined inscription including date, ETO
       IΘBAA ΓΡΙΠΠ (Year 19 of King Agrippa). Struck 75 C.E.
                                                               300.00
88a.   AE 12mm.
       O: Veiled head of Livia to right, inscription around, CEBACTH
       (Augusta).
       R: Upside down anchor, date in field LIΘ BA (Year 19 =
       79/80 C.E., King Agrippa). AJC II, 253, 21.   400.00
89.   AE 23mm.
       O: Laureate bust of Domitian right, inscription around, ΔΟΜΕΤΙ
       KAICAP ΓΕΡΜ (Caesar Domitian Germanicus).
       R: Nike advances right, holding wreath in right hand and palm
       branch over shoulder in left; in field, Greek inscription and date,
       ETO KΔBA ΑΓΡΙΠΠΑ (Year 24 of King Agrippa). Struck
       80 C.E. AJC II, 253, 22.   350.00

90   91

90.   AE 19mm.
O: Laureate bust of Domitian right; inscription around,   ΔOMIT ΚΑΙCΑP ΓΕΡΜΑΝ.
R: Inscription of three lines,   ETO   ΚΔΒΑΑ   ΓΡΙΠΠ   (Year 24 of King Agrippa), within wreath and border of dots. Struck 80 C.E. AJC II, 253, 23.   400.00

91.   AE 16mm.
O: Laureate bust of Domitian right; inscription around;   ΔOMET-ΚΑΙC   ΓΕΡΜ.
R: Eight-branched palm tree with two bunches of dates; inscription and date across field,   ET   KE   BAC   ΑΓΡΙΠ   (Year 25 of King Agrippa). Struck 81 C.E. AJC II, 254, 28.   500.00

93   94

92.   AE 11mm.
O: Laureate bust of Domitian right, inscription around,   ΔOMIT

R: Single cornucopia with date and inscription across field,   ETKE BA   ΑΓ   (Year 25 of King Agrippa). Struck 81 C.E. AJC II, 254, 29.   250.00

93.   AE 20mm.
O: Laureate bust of Domitian right; inscription around,   ΔOMIT-IANOC   ΚΑΙCΑP.
R: Nike stands right resting foot on helmet and writing on shield resting on her knee; inscription and date around,   ETO   KZBA ΑΓΡΙΠΠΑ   (Year 27 of King Agrippa). Struck 83 C.E. AJC II, 256, 42.   275.00

94.   AE 17mm.
O: Laureate bust of Domitian right, inscription around,   ΔOMIT-IANOC   ΚΑΙCΑP.
R: Double cornucopias crossed at base; inscription and date between horns and around,   BA   ΑΓΡΙΠΠΑ   ETO   KZ   (Year 27 of King Agrippa). Struck 83 C.E. AJC II, 256, 43.   400.00

95

96   97

95. AE 20/21mm.
O: Laureate bust of Domitian right; inscription (in Latin) around, IM CA D VES F DOM AV GER COS XII. (Emperor Caesar, son of divine Vespasian, Domitian Augustus Germanicus, Consul for the 12th time).
R: Large SC surrounded by inscription (Greek) and date, ΕΠΙ ΒΑ ΑΓΡΙ ΕΤ ΚΣ (By King Agrippa, Year 26). Struck 87 C.E. AJC II, 255, 36.   300.00

96. AE 19/20mm.
O: Laureate bust of Domitian right, inscription around (Latin), IM CA D VES F DOM AV GER COS XII.
R: Double cornucopias crossed at base, winged caduceus between, inscription and date above and across field, ΕΠΙΒΑ ΑΓΡΙ (By King Agrippa, Year 26), SC in exergue. Struck 87 C.E. AJC II, 255, 35.   500.00

97. AE 12mm.
O: Bust of Tyche right, inscription on right, ΒΑ ΑΓΡ (King Agrippa).
R: Single cornucopia with date in field, ΕΤΛΔ (Year 34). Struck 90 C.E. AJC II, 258, 52.   250.00

98. AE 26mm.
O: Laureate bust of Domitian right, inscription around, ΑΥΤΟΚΡΛ ΔΟΜΙΤΙΑ ΚΑΙCΑΡ ΓΕΡΜΑΝΙ (Emperor Domitian Caesar Germanicus).
R: Tyche stands left on platform holding cornucopia in left hand and ears of barley in right; inscription and date across field, ΕΤΟΥ ΕΛΒΑ ΑΓΡΙΠΠΑ (Year 35 of King Agrippa). Struck 91 C.E. AJC II, 258, 53.   550.00

98

99. AE 15mm.
O: Laureate bust of Domitian right, inscription around, ΑΥΤΟΚ-ΔΟΜ.
R: Inscription and date in two lines, ΒΑΑΓΡ ΕΤΕΛ (King Agrippa, Year 35), surrounded by wreath. Struck 91 C.E. AJC II, 258, 56.   300.00

6. PROCURATORS OF JUDAEA UNDER ROME: 6–66 C.E.

And after certain days, when Felix came with his wife Drusilla, which was a Jewess, he sent for Paul, and heard him concerning the faith in Christ. (Acts 24:24)

But after two years Porcius Festus came into Felix' room: and Felix, willing to show the Jews a pleasure, left Paul bound. (Acts 24:27)

And when they had bound him, they led him away, and delivered him to Pontius Pilate the governor. (Matthew 27:2)

Following the exile of Herod Archelaus in 6 C.E., Judaea was annexed to the Roman province of Syria. The Emperor Augustus appointed Coponius to the post of procurator, or governor, over Judaea. He was the first of 14 men to hold this position. With the exception of the three years Agrippa I reigned as king (41–44 C.E.) the procurators ruled until 66 C.E., when the First Revolt erupted. The procurators resided at Caesarea, the magnificent harbor city built by Herod I. Unlike the governors of Syria, the procurators of Judaea were not former senators or others of aristocratic rank, but were from lower social classes.

Coponius, the first procurator, began his rule by calling for a census of the Jews for the purpose of imposing stiff taxes. And the procurators who followed Coponius were no bargains for the Jews either. Pontius Pilatus (Pilate), in particular, strained relations with the Jewish people.

The procurators who took power after the short reign of Agrippa I were even worse than their predecessors. Of one of them, Felix, who rose to the post of procurator from slavery, Tacitus wrote: "He exercised the prerogative of a king in the spirit of a slave, with superlative cruelty and licentiousness."

Of another, Albinus, Josephus wrote, "Not only did he embezzle public moneys and rob a multitude of private citizens of their property and burden the whole people with imposts, but he released captive highwaymen for ransoms from their relatives . . . Every villain gathered a band of his own, and Albinus towered among them like a robber-chief, using his adherents to plunder honest citizens. The victims remained silent; others, still exempt, flattered the wretch in order to secure immunity.

"Nevertheless, Albinus appeared honorable in comparison with his successor, Gessius Florus. For while the former had practiced his villainies in secret, and with a certain degree of caution, Gessius Florus made an open boast of his crimes against the people; he practiced every sort of robbery and abuse precisely as though he had been sent to punish condemned criminals. His cruelty was pitiless, his infamies shameless; never before did anyone so veil truth with deceit, or discover more cunning ways of accomplishing his knaveries . . . he robbed whole cities and ruined whole communities . . . Whole districts were depopulated by his greed, multitudes left their homes and fled into foreign provinces."

Florus's abuses of the Jews mounted one on the other, antagonizing and punishing them until they could stand no more. The final insult came when Florus demanded 17 talents from the Temple treasury for his own use. (In 1962, in his book *Jews, God, and History*, Max Dimont estimated 17 talents to be worth $350,000. Today, taking inflation into consideration, the figure would be more like $750,000.) In their outrage, bands of sarcastic Jews took to the streets with signs begging pennies for "the poor, destitute Florus." This mockery enraged the procurator, who called upon his troops to sack the upper city; more than 600 Jews were killed.

His treachery was so great that even Berenice, sister of Agrippa II, who happened to be in Jerusalem at the time, went barefoot to Florus and implored mercy for the Jews. But he insulted and ridiculed her and drove her away.

Then, to prevent Florus from plundering the Temple, the Jews destroyed all the approaches and bridges to the holy site.

At this time the Jews gathered around Agrippa II, who was a Jew after all, and begged him to denounce Florus to Nero. Agrippa demanded that first the people restore the broken connections to the Temple and pay the back taxes they owed to Rome. The Jews met both demands, but balked when Agrippa said they ought to honor Florus as the representative of Rome until he was replaced. At this suggestion Agrippa was pelted with stones and he quickly left the city.

In their distaste for Florus, and subsequent discontent with Rome, the Jews decided to cease the daily sacrifice for the emperor in the Temple, a tradition going back to the time of Augustus. With this action, war was declared.

With the exception of the coins of Pontius Pilatus, the coins of the procurators do not carry symbols abhorrent to the Jews. Pilatus' coins expressed his total lack of understanding toward the Jews, and carried pagan cult symbols such as the littus and simpulum (libation ladle). Otherwise the coins of the procurators generally carry agricultural symbols, amphora, or goblet. One coin of Felix does show crossed shields and spears, and may have shown the "constant friction and strained relations between him and the Jewish masses," according to Meshorer.

The Procurators of Judaea under Rome

Under Augustus

Coponius (6–9 C.E.)
Marcus Ambibulus (9–12 C.E.)
*Annius Rufus (12–15 C.E.)

Under Tiberius

Valerius Gratus (15–26 C.E.)
Pontius Pilatus (26–36 C.E.)
*Marcellus (36–37 C.E.)

Under Caligula

*Marullus (37–41 C.E.)

Under Claudius

*Cuspius Fadus (44–46 C.E.)
*Tiberius Alexander (46–48 C.E.)
*Ventidius Cumanus (48–54 C.E.)
Antonius Felix (52–54 C.E.)

Under Nero

Antonius Felix (54–59 C.E.)
Porcius Festus (59–62 C.E.)
*Albinus (62–64 C.E.)
*Gessius Florus (64–66 C.E.)
(*apparently issued no coins)

Procurators

Coponius (6–9 C.E.) under Augustus

100.   AE 15/17mm.
O: Ear of barley curved to right, Greek inscription   KAICAPOC
(Caesar).
R: Eight-branched palm tree bearing two bunches of dates, date in
field LΛS (Year 36). Struck 6 C.E. AJC II, Supp. V, 1.40.00

Marcus Ambibulus (9–12 C.E.) under Augustus

101.   AE 16mm.
O: Ear of barley curved to right, Greek inscription   KAICAPOC.
R: Eight-branched palm tree bearing two bunches of dates, date in
field LΛΘ (Year 39). Struck 9 C.E. AJC II, Supp. V, 3.
40.00

102   103

102. AE 17mm.
      O: Same as no. 101.
      R: Eight-branched palm tree bearing two bunches of dates, date in
         field LM   (Year 40). Struck 10 C.E. AJC II, Supp. V, 4.
                                                                  50.00

103. AE 15/17mm.
      O: Same as no. 101.
      R: Eight-branched palm tree bearing two bunches of dates, date in
         field LMA   (Year 41). Struck 11 C.E. AJC II, Supp. V, 5.
                                                                  40.00

Valerius Gratus (15–26 C.E.) under Tiberius

104   105

104. AE 15.5mm.
      O: Greek inscription KAI CAP within a wreath.
      R: Double cornucopias with Greek inscription TIB (Tiberius)
         and date LB (Year two) between horns. Struck 15 C.E. AJC
         II, Supp. V, 6.   90.00

105. AE 16mm.
      O: Greek inscription IOY ΛIA (Julia—refers to Julia Livia,
         mother of Tiberius) within a wreath.
      R: Palm branch flanked by date LB (Year two). Struck 15 C.E.
         AJC II, Supp. V, 8.   125.00

   A variety of this coin occurs with the inscription KAI CAP on the
obverse.

106. **AE 13/16mm.**
   O: Greek inscription KAI CAP within a wreath.
   R: Two crossed cornucopias with caduceus between them, Greek inscription above TIBEPIOY, date in field LΓ (Year three). AJC II, Supp. V, 10.   75.00

107. **AE 15mm.**
   O: Greek inscription IOY ΛIA within a wreath.
   R: Three lilies in bloom flanked by date LΓ (Year three). Struck 16 C.E. AJC II, Supp. V, 12.   75.00
   A rare variety of this coin occurs with the inscription KAI CAP on obverse (107a).

108. **AE 16.5mm.**
   O: Vine leaf and small bunch of grapes with Greek inscription above IOYΛIA.
   R: Narrow-necked amphora with scroll handles, flanked by date LΔ (Year four). Struck 17 C.E. AJC II, Supp. V, 16.   150.00

109. **AE 15/17mm.**
   O: Vine leaf on branch with Greek inscription above TIBEPIOC.
   R: Kantharos with scroll handles, flanked by date LΔ (Year four), Greek inscription above KAICAP. Struck 17 C.E. AJC II, Supp. V, 15.   200.00

110. **AE 16mm.**
   O: Greek inscription TIB KAI CAP (Tiberius Caesar) within wreath tied at bottom with an X.
   R: Palm branch curves to right flanked by Greek inscription IOYΛIA and date LΔ (Year four). Struck 17 C.E. AJC II, Supp. V, 17.   50.00

111   112

111. AE 15.5mm.
      O: Same as no. 110.
      R: Palm branch curves to right flanked by Greek inscription
      IOYΛIA and date LE (Year five). Struck 18 C.E. AJC II,
      Supp. V, 18.   40.00

112. AE 15/17mm.
      O: Same as no. 110.
      R: Palm branch curves to right flanked by Greek inscription
      IOYΛIA and date LIA (Year 11). Struck 24 C.E. AJC II,
      Supp. V, 19   40.00

Pontius Pilatus (26–36 C.E.) under Tiberius

113   114

113. AE 16mm.
      O: Three bound ears of barley, the outer two ears droop, sur-
      rounded by Greek inscription IOYΛIA KAICAPOC.
      R: Libation ladle (simpulum) surrounded by Greek inscription
      TIBEPIOY KAICAPOC (of Tiberius Caesar) and date LIS
      (Year 16). Struck 29 C.E. AJC II, Supp. V, 21.   75.00

114. AE 15.5mm.
      O: Littus surrounded by Greek inscription, TIBEPIOY KAI-
      CAPOC.
      R: Date within wreath LIZ (Year 17). Struck 30 C.E. AJC II,
      Supp. V, 23.   60.00
      This coin is also found with the date LIS; the Z apparently is in
retrograde. Some believe, however, that this is really LIS (Year 16) or 29
C.E. *(114a).*

114a   115

115.   AE 14/16mm.
      O: Littus surrounded by Greek inscription.   TIBEPIOY KAI-
         CAPOC.
      R: Date within wreath   LIH   (Year 18). Struck 31 C.E. AJC II,
         Supp. V, 24.   65.00

*Dates such as   LH   and others sometimes seem to appear on these coins,
and it is a matter of controversy whether these are additional dates or simply
carelessly engraved dies.*

Antonius Felix (52–59 C.E.) under Claudius

116   117

116.   AE 17.6mm.
      O: Greek inscription IOY ΛIAAΓ PIΠΠI NA (Julia Agrip-
         pina—wife of Claudius) within a wreath tied at bottom with an
         X.
      R: Two crossed palm branches, Greek inscription around, TI
         KΛAVΔIOC KAICAP ΓEPM (Tiberius Claudius Caesar
         Germanicus), date below, LIΔ (Year 14). Struck 54 C.E. AJC
         II, Supp. V, 32.   50.00

117.   AE 16.5mm.
      O: Two oblong shields and two spears crossed surrounded by Greek
         inscription, NEPW KΛAV KAICAP (Nero Claudius Cae-
         sar—son of Claudius).
      R: Six-branched palm tree bearing two bunches of dates, Greek
         inscription above and below, BPIT (Brittanicus—second son
         of Claudius), date in field, LIΔ/KAI (Year 14). Struck 54 C.E.
         AJC II, Supp. V, 29.   50.00

Porcius Festus (59–62 C.E) under Nero

118   118v

118.   AE 17mm.
   O: Greek inscription within a wreath tied at bottom with an X,
      NEP WNO C (Nero).
   R: Palm branch surrounded by Greek inscription KAIC APOC
      and date LE (Year five). Struck 58 C.E. AJC II, Supp. V,
      35.   40.00
   This coin sometimes occurs with various retrograde inscriptions
(*Varieties*).   50.00

7. THE FIRST REVOLT: 66–70 C.E.

The war of the Jews against Rome did not begin suddenly. Ever since the death of Agrippa I and the ensuing rule of the first Roman procurator, there had been many clashes of short duration between Romans and Jews. Even in relatively quiet times the land seethed with rebellion.

The insults of the procurator Florus finally caused the explosion of Judaea against its Roman oppressors. In spite of pleading by Agrippa II, who was in Jerusalem at the time, the Jews refused to take any more of Florus's mistreatment. Agrippa also warned that Jews around the world would "be devastated by the enemy if you rebel."

Even though several factions of Jews continued to fight among themselves, in May of the year 66 C.E. they united sufficiently to rout the Roman garrisons stationed in and around Jerusalem.

These initial Jewish victories sent shock waves throughout the Roman Empire. True to Agrippa II's prediction, Jews everywhere were murdered. In Caesarea more than 20,000 Jews were massacred in a single bloody hour. In Damascus 10,000 more were killed. And in Antioch, Alexandria, and other cities there was similar carnage.

The Romans knew that the rebellion of this tiny nation had to be stamped out quickly, lest other provinces get the wrong idea about the strength of the empire.

From their position in nearby Syria came Rome's 12th Legion under general Cestus Gallus, who aimed to quiet the embattled Jews. But the troops were successfully repelled. When word of this defeat reached Nero in Rome, he knew how dangerous the situation had become. He called upon his most distinguished general, the aging Flavius Vespasian, who had led Rome's armies to victory in Germany and Britain.

Given the best of Rome's fighting forces and virtually unlimited power, Vespasian departed for Palestine. When he arrived his first move was to encircle Galilee, where the Jewish forces were under the command of one Joseph ben Matthias. Galilee fell within a few months, but before it did, this Joseph surrendered to Vespasian and tried to convince his fellows to do the same. They did not. Meanwhile, Joseph befriended Vespasian and became a court follower and historian—known today as Flavius Josephus, the only Jewish historian of that time whose works survive today.

By the middle of the year 68 Vespasian's troops had succeeded in crushing the revolt throughout Palestine. Only Jerusalem and the zealot fortress Massada remained. Massada, for now, was ignored, and Vespasian prepared to besiege Jerusalem. But at about this time Nero died and civil wars rocked Rome. The Eastern legions proclaimed Vespasian emperor, and within a year he victoriously claimed the throne in Rome. He had not forgotton the Jews, however, nor his desire to crush their uprising once and for all, and he sent his son Titus to finish the job he had started.

Within Jerusalem the three factions of Jews continued to battle; the zealots under Eleazar, the Sicarii (or knife-men) under Simon ben Giora, and their opposition led by John of Gishala.

Titus's siege machines pounded the city and its walls with battering rams and huge stones. Even while Titus was at work on the outside of Jerusalem his allies, famine and plague, struck down thousands of the besieged Jews. Slowly but surely Titus's men and machines tore down the city's three walls.

When the last wall fell the survivors holed up in the Temple compound and continued to resist for six more days. It is said that Titus had ordered the Temple itself saved, but as his troops smelled the success that had so long eluded them, they burnt it to the ground and butchered its protectors. Even after this, however, isolated pockets of resistance flickered in the Temple area, and it was a month before all were wiped out.

Few realize that throughout all of this at least four ranking Jews stood with Titus: the apostate Tiberius Alexander, of Alexandria, who was a former procurator of Judaea, was his chief of staff; Agrippa II, who commanded a large army of auxiliaries; Berenice, sister of Agrippa II, who was the mistress of Titus and hoped to become his wife; and the turncoat historian, Josephus, who chronicled the campaign.

Upon Titus's final victory, Josephus wrote of the Jewish captives: "The tallest and handsomest of the youths were reserved for the triumphal procession in Rome. Of the rest, all over 17 were given by Titus to various provinces for gladiatorial combats with men and beasts. Those under 17 were sold. The total number of prisoners taken throughout the war amounted to 97,000. And those who perished during the entire siege from the war, pestilence and famine numbered 1,100,000."

The golden Menorah and other holy implements of the Temple were taken to Rome and put in the Roman Temple of Peace. They have long since disppeared, but we are reminded of them even today by the reliefs on the arch that Titus had built in Rome to commemorate his victory over the tiny Jewish nation. That arch stands today not as a monument to its Roman builders, whose civilization is long gone, but as a monument to the Jewish people who outlived their conquerers by many generations.

Actually, the Jewish revolt had not yet been entirely crushed. For three more years a band of zealots held out at the mountain fortress of Massada near the Dead Sea. And even when this last heroic bastion of freedom fell, the Jewish people did not. Their faith depended more on traditions and laws than on the sanctuary and sacrifices. Virtually at the moment of Rome's victory, Rabbi Johanan ben Zakki, with Titus's blessing, was establishing a center of learning in the city of Jabneh.

The coins of the First Revolt were a significant expression of the Jews' freedom from Rome, for they struck not only coins of bronze, but coins of silver as well—a privilege usually reserved strictly for the emperor. Coins of the First Revolt are dated from years one to five, corresponding to the five years (actually just more than four) of the war. The coins carry "revolutionary" slogans such as "for the freedom of Zion," and "for the redemption of Zion," as well as "Jerusalem the Holy." Symbols on the coins of the First Revolt are characteristically Jewish: the lulav etrog. chalice, amphora, three pomegranates, vine leaf, and palm tree. All inscriptions on the coins of the First Revolt are in the ancient Hebrew script.

The Thick Silver Shekels

The shekel is among the most fabled and historically significant of all the ancient coins, even if not the most ornate or beautiful. That honor would have to go to the sophisticated coins of the Greeks, issued hundreds of years before our modest silver shekel. But the Jewish shekel is beautiful in its simplicity and in its symbolism. And when one considers the strife under which our shekel was conceived, designed, and issued, one will have an even greater appreciation of the coin.

The obverse shows a chalice with the ancient Hebrew inscription, "Shekel of Israel," with the date in Hebrew letters above the chalice. The reverse shows a stem with three pomegranates and carries the inscription "Jerusalem the holy." Jewish shekels weigh approximately 14 grams, and the edges have been hammered (peened) uniformly, except on the specimens of the first year which are somewhat cruder.

Controversies raged over these shekels for hundreds of years. Once most scholars were of the belief that the "thick Jewish shekels," as they were called in the late 1800s and early 1900s, were actually issued by Simon Maccabee, who was at one time granted permission by Antiochus VII Sidetes, Seleucid ruler of Syria, to mint coins of his own for the land of Judaea.

Today, however, we are certain that Simon never actually issued coins, since Antiochus revoked his grant. At any rate, archaeological and historical evidence have by this time absolutely proven that the silver Jewish shekels date from the First Revolt.

The war lasted for less than five years—but it spanned five different years. Hence the shekels were issued with five different dates, from year one to year five. The rarest of these was issued in the fifth year, next in rarity the fourth, then the first.

Large silver coins of Bar Kochba, with a lulav and etrog on the obverse, and the Temple facade on the reverse, are sometimes also referred to as "shekels." In fact, however, these are better described as "tetradrachms," or "*sela*," as the Talmud calls them.

One fascinating fact about the Jewish shekels of the First Revolt is that nobody knows who issued them. The war against Rome was a time of both internal strife among the Jews, as well as war against the Roman legions, led first by Vespasian and later by his son Titus.

At the time the war began the Jews were split into several factions, and to this date it is not really known which one of these factions—or perhaps some central governing body—actually issued the coins.

It is obvious because of their date of issue that the Jewish shekels could not have been the "thirty pieces of silver" supposedly paid to Judas.

The Temple Tribute and Other Jewish Rituals

According to the Mishnah and other sources, the Temple tribute was payable only in Tyrian coinage, and this included the annual half-shekel that every Israelite had to pay to the Temple.

> *The five* selas *due for the [Firstborn] son should be paid in Tyrian coinage; the thirty due for the slave [that was gored by an ox] and the fifty due from the violator and the seducer, and the hundred due from him that* hath brought up an evil name, *are all to be paid according to the value of the shekels of the sanctuary, in Tyrian coinage. Aught that is to be redeemed may be redeemed with silver or its value, save only the Shekel-dues.* (Mishnah, *Bekhoroth* 8:7)

There is a further discussion and description of the Tyrian shekels in Chapter 11.

First Revolt

שקל ישראל א

ירושלם קדשה

119

119.   AR, 13.51gm.
      O: Chalice with smooth rim, pearl on either side, the base is flat with pearled ends; Hebrew inscription (shekel of Israel) and date (aleph) "Year 1" above chalice.
      R: Stem with pearled base and three fruits, perhaps pomegranates, surrounded by Hebrew inscription (Jerusalem the holy). AJC II, 259, 3.   2,500.00
The weight of the silver shekels and half-shekels is fairly standard, as is their fabric; the coins are quite thick and their edges always hammered. The ends of the letters of the inscriptions are pearled.   2,500.00

� PWℲ ⱶ⅄ᗺ

חצי השקל

120

120. AR, 6.61gm.
   O: Chalice with smooth rim, pearl on either sie, the base is flat
   with pearled ends; Hebrew inscription (half a shekel) and date
   (aleph) "Year 1": above chalice.
   R: Same as no. 119. AJC II, 259, 6.   2,000.000

120a. AR, 3.28gm.
   O: Chalice as no. 120; Hebrew inscription (quarter of a shekel) and
   date (aleph) "Year 1" above.
   R: Same as no. 120. AJC II, 260, 7.   EXTREMELY RARE

ᘔW ∠F ⅂W⅄ ⱶPW

שקל ישראל שב

ℲWⳆⱶPℲ ⱨ⅄ⳆWⱵⴹⱵ

ירושלים הקדשה

121

121. AR, 14.08gm.
   O: Chalice with pearled rim, the base is raised by projections on
   ends: Hebrew inscription (shekel of Israel) and date (shin bet)
   "Year 2" above chalice.
   R: Stem with pearled bottom and three fruits, perhaps pomegran-
   ates, surrounded by Hebrew inscription (Jerusalem the holy).
   AJC II, 260, 8.   1,350.00

ⳆTWℲ ⱶ⅄ᗺ

חצי השקל

122

122. AR, 6.70gm.
   O: Chalice with pearled rim, the base is raised by projections on
   ends; Hebrew inscription (half a shekel) and date (shin bet)
   "Year 2" above chalice.
   R: Same as no. 121. AJC II, 260, 10.   1,450.00

שַׁאֲתַ שֵׁאֲתַ

שנת שתים

חרוּת ציון

חרות ציון

123. AE 17.5mm.
      O: Amphora with broad rim and two handles, surrounded by He-
      brew inscription (year two).
      R: Vine leaf on small branch, surrounded by inscription (the free-
      dom of Zion). AJC II, 260, 12.   55.00

*This coin, to many the classic Jewish small bronze, occurs in dozens of
fascinating varieties. Among these are the "Barbarous imitations," which
Kadman says were likely "struck by Jewish detachments outside Jerusalem.
We know, for instance, from Josephus that during the second year and half
of the third year of the war, Simon bar Giora succeeded in gathering considerable forces and that he occupied or reconquered important parts of
southern Judaea and of Idumaea. It seems possible that, while not daring
to imitate the 'holy' silver Shekel, he issued small bronze coins of pruta
denomination from the prototype of the coins: year two—freedom of Zion.
But since he had no experienced and skilled die-cutters like those of the
Jerusalem mint, there emerged the prutot of year two, erroneously considered
later to be 'barbarous' imitations." It is also possible, however, that these
barbaric coins were engraved and struck by unskilled workers at the main
mint. One of these interesting barbarous coins follows.*

123a. AE 17.3mm.
      O: Crude amphora surrounded by barbaric inscription copying no.
      123.
      R: Crude vine leaf surrounded by barbaric inscription copying no.
      123. Struck 67 C.E. AJC II, 261, 13c.   65.00

שר

שג

124. AR, 14.23gm.
      O: Chalice with pearled rim, the base is raised by projections on
      ends; Hebrew inscription around, (shekel of Israel) and date
      (shin gimel) "Year 3" above chalice.
      R: Same as no. 121. AJC II, 261, 18.   1,450.00

125.   AR, 6.98gm.
O: Chalice with pearled rim, the base is raised by projections on
ends; Hebrew inscription around, (half a shekel) and date (shin
gimel) above chalice.
R: Same as no. 121. AJC II, 261, 19.   1,450.00

ᴪꙶᴄᴧ Ӿꚍꝯꟼ
חרות ציון

Wꚍ∠W XꙶW
שנת שלוש

126.   AE 16.2mm.
O: Amphora with broad rim, two handles, and lid decorated with
tiny globes hanging around edge, surrounded by Hebrew inscription (year three).
R: Vine leaf on small branch, surrounded by inscription (the freedom of Zion). AJC II, 261, 20.   65.00

*This coin is generally found in poorer quality than its year-two cousin,
with the barbarous imitations being exceedingly rare in this, the third year.
The description of what may be a barbarous imitation, with a retrograde
inscription, follows.*

126a.   AE 15.4mm.
O: Barbaric amphora surrounded by crude inscription, probably
retrograde (year three).
R: Barbaric vine leaf surrounded by totally schematic inscription. Similar to AJC II, 261, 13c.   55.00

*Since this specimen is struck off center and neither the amphora nor the
inscription is complete, it is problematic whether this is actually a retrograde
year three specimen.*

ᐊW
שד

127.   AR, 14.05gm.
O: Chalice with pearled rim, the base is raised by projections on
ends; Hebrew inscription around, (shekel of Israel) and date
(shin daled) "Year 4" above chalice.
R: Same as no. 121. AJC II, 262, 23.   10,000.00

128.

128.   AR, 6.98gm.
　　　　O: Chalice with pearled rim, the base is raised by projections on
　　　　　　ends; Hebrew inscription around, (half a shekel) and date (shin
　　　　　　gimel) "Year 4" above chalice.
　　　　R: Same as no. 121. AJC II, 262, 25.　　　　　　　　　　55,000.00
　　*In purchasing the shekel of the fourth year the buyer must beware that
the specimen is not merely a coin of the second year with the lower portion
of the "bet" removed to appear as if it were a "daled."*
　　*(The unique, and controversial, silver quarter shekel of the fourth year is
not listed.)*

שנת ארבע חצי

לגאלת ציון

129.

129.   AE 26mm.
　　　　O: Etrog flanked by a lulav on either side, surrounded by Hebrew
　　　　　　inscription, (year four—half).
　　　　R: Seven-branched palm tree with two bunches of dates, flanked
　　　　　　by baskets of fruit; surrounded by Hebrew inscription (to the
　　　　　　redemption of Zion). Struck 69 C.E. at Jerusalem. AJC II, 262,
　　　　　　27.　　　　　　　　　　　　　　　　　　　　　　　　4,000.00
　　*The lulav, consisting of myrtle, palm branch, and willow tied together,
as well as the etrog, are used in the celebration of the holiday Succoth, the
Feast of the Tabernacles.*

לגאלת ציון

שנת ארבע רביע

130

130. AE 22.2mm.
      O: Two lulavs surrounded by Hebrew inscription (year four—
      quarter).
      R: Etrog surrounded by Hebrew inscription (to the redemption of
      Zion). Struck 69 C.E. at Jerusalem. AJC II, 262, 29.   1,750.00

131

שנת ארבע

לגאלת ציון

131. AE 20mm.
      O: Lulav flanked by an etrog on either side surrounded by Hebrew
      inscription (year four).
      R: Chalice with pearled rim surrounded by Hebrew inscription (to
      the redemption of Zion). Struck 69 C.E. at Jerusalem. AJC II,
      262, 30.   200.00
131a. AE 20mm.
      O: Lulav flanked by an etrog on either side surrounded by Hebrew
      inscription (year four).
      R: Chalice with pearled rim surrounded by Hebrew inscription in
      retrograde (to the redemption of Zion). Struck 69 C.E. AJC II,
      263, 30d.   275.00
*With its crude workmanship and retrograde inscription, it is possible that
this coin was struck by Jewish troops outside of Jerusalem.*

שה

132

132. AR, 13.87gm.
      O: Chalice with pearled rim, the base is raised by projections on
      ends; Hebrew inscription around, (Shekel of Israel) and date
      shin heh) "Year 5" above chalice.
      R: Same as no. 121. Struck 70 C.E. at Jerusalem. AJC II, 263,
      31.
*In 1983 a shekel of year five in extremely fine condition sold at public
auction for $155,000.00.*

8. BAR KOCHBA: 132–135 C.E.

There shall step forth a star out of Jacob, And a sceptre shall rise out of Israel. (Numbers 24:17)

Simon bar Kosiba, President over Israel, to Yehonathan and Masabala, peace. [My order is] that you search and seize the wheat which is in the possession of Hanun. (Bar Kochba's Letters, "The Wooden Letter")

After the Jews were expelled from Jerusalem by Titus and his troops, and the warriors of Massada finally fell, a new Diaspora grew throughout the ancient world. New refugees from the Holy Land bolstered Jewish communities already in exile. Emotionally as well as practically, the Diaspora Jews of this time looked toward the day that their Temple would be rebuilt and they would return to the holy Jerusalem.

These feelings simmered under the surface for decades, until just more than 40 years after the fall of the second Temple, when they boiled over. From 115 to 117 C.E. the Jews, primarily those living in the Diaspora, began a series of revolts, which probably also reached the Jews remaining in the Land of Israel.

The revolt of the Jews in Mesopotamia was crushed by the Roman general L. Quietus, who later was made governor of the Land of Israel. This series of revolts, therefore, became known as the "War of Quietus."

By 132 C.E. a new revolt of the Jews arose, but this time it was fought again in the Land of Israel, where the fervent followers of the Jewish faith went "underground" both figuratively and literally and began to torment the Romans once again. The spiritual leader of this revolt was Rabbi Akiba, and the military leader was one Simon Ben Kosiba, also known as Simon Bar Kochba.

Akiba recognized Bar Kochba as the Messiah. But many colleagues did not agree. Rabbi Johanan Ben Tortha told Akiba, "Grass will grow in your jawbones and He (the Messiah) will still not have come."

The Bar Kochba Revolt probably arose because of a combination of factors. First the proclamations by Hadrian that he would rename and rebuild Jerusalem as Aelia Capitolina. In another proclamation, possibly not aimed directly at the Jews, but affecting them, Hadrian forbade castration of males (as several emperors had done before him); ignorant of Jewish customs, Hadrian also put circumcision in this category, and it was punishable by death. Furthermore, one must remember that many Jews of this period remained preoccupied with regaining Jerusalem and rebuilding the Temple and its cult to former splendor.

Coins of Bar Kochba with the inscription "Eleazar the priest" indicate that restoration of the Temple and its ritual use was one of Bar Kochba's prime considerations.

Bar Kochba was apparently a brilliant warrior in the tradition of Judah

Maccabee. One story relates that Bar Kochba wanted only the bravest, strongest men in his army. To test each of them he would cut off a part of his little finger. But the Sages sent him a message asking, "How long will you continue to make the men of Israel blemished?"

Bar Kochba replied, "How else shall they be tested?"

The Sages replied: "Let anyone who cannot uproot a cedar from Lebanon be refused enrollment in your army."

Bar Kochba agreed to the change in procedures. It is said that Bar Kochba himself was a great warrior. Once when he went into battle he implored his Lord to "Neither help us nor discourage us!"

And when his enemies hit him with their missiles, "He would catch the missiles from the enemy's catapults on one of his knees and hurl them back, killing many of the foe. On that account R. Akiba made his remark."

Saint Jerome wrote that Bar Kochba gave the impression that he was "spewing out flames," by "fanning a lighted blade of straw in his mouth with puffs of breath".

When Hadrian called upon his general Julius Severus and sent him to the Land of Israel, he began to slowly smother the flames Bar Kochba had ignited. The Roman historian Dio Cassius reports that "Very few of [the Jews] in fact survived. Fifty of their most important outposts and nine hundred and eighty-five of their most famous villages were razed to the ground. Five hundred and eighty thousand men were slain in the various raids and battles, and the number of those that perished by famine, disease and fire was past finding out."

Dio Cassius doesn't report in the same detail the severity of the struggle on the side of the Romans. He does note, however, that "Many Romans . . . perished in this war." Just how many can be seen by his next sentence: "Therefore Hadrian in writing to the senate did not employ the opening phrase commonly affected by the emperors, 'If you and your children are in health, it is well; I and the legions are in health.' "

Thus another brief flicker of freedom was extinguished for the Jewish people.

"From now on," Ya'akov Meshorer notes, "Judaism contracted itself within the limits of the four cubits of the Torah, and the earthly Jerusalem gave place to the heavenly Jerusalem."

The coins of Bar Kochba, although issued in a period of severe economic and political stress, are the most beautiful of all ancient Jewish coins. Notable designs include the musical instruments used in the Temple service, as well as the sacred vessels used there. The facade of the Temple, etrog and lulav, palm tree, branch, grapes, and vine leaves were also depicted on the coins of Bar Kochba.

He apparently learned from the Romans the propaganda value of coins, and had his coins struck with slogans designed to keep the spark of hope kindled among his people: "Year one of the redemption of Israel," "Year two of the freedom of Israel," "For the freedom of Jerusalem," and a simple, hopeful, "Jerusalem." "Simon," Bar Kochba's first name, also appeared on the coins, and he sometimes styles himself "Prince of Israel."

The coins of Bar Kochba were not struck on cast planchets, but on Roman, Syrian, and other local coins. The foreign coins were prepared by hammering (the silver coins) or both hammering and filing (for the bronze) to remove traces of the hated alien symbols. Traces of the original coin can almost always be seen on the silver coins, and file marks are not uncommon on the bronzes. Rarely, an imperial portrait and a few letters from the original coin remain on bronze coins of this period.

There were an extremely large number of coin types struck during the Bar Kochba years. These were created by interchanging dies, thus producing many different combinations, some of which are not shown here. By studying the plates and sketches, particularly of the denarii, the reader will see how a few dies can combine in many different ways.

In the Mishna the large silver tetradrachm of Bar Kochba is referred to as a *sela*, and the denarius as a *zuz*.

Bar Kochba

Coins of the First Year (132–133 C.E.)

133. AR tetradrachm, 14.81gm.
   O: Facade of the Temple in Jerusalem with ark and scrolls (viewed from end) in center, surrounded by inscription (Jerusalem).
   R: Lulav with etrog at left, surrounded by Hebrew inscription (year one of the redemption of Israel). AJC II, 264, 1.   15,000.00

134. AR denarius, 3.17gm.
   O: Jug with handle, palm branch at right, surrounded by inscription (Eleazer the priest).
   R: Inscription within a wreath (Shim). AJC II, 267, 17.   2,750.00

The abbreviation "Shim" can also be read "Shma" because of the order of the letters. Some numismatists have contended that indeed there is a dual meaning in this use of the first three letters of Bar Kochba's first name; first, a simple abbreviation, and second as the first word of the prayer, the Shema, which they believe was one of Bar Kochba's rallying cries.

ירו
שלם

שנת אחת לגאלת ישראל

135.   AE 32mm.
    O: Amphora with two handles, surrounded by inscription (year one of the redemption of Israel).
    R: Inscription (Jerusalem) surrounded by a wreath. AJC II, 264, 4.   4,500.00

שמעון נשיא
ישראל

136.   AE 34mm.
    O: Amphora with two handles, surrounded by inscription (year one of the redemption of Israel)
    R: Inscription (Simon Prince of Israel) within a wreath. AJC II, 264, 3.   3,500.00

137.   AE 23.6mm.
    O: Seven-branched palm tree with two bunches of dates; across field below, inscription (Simon Prince of Israel).
    R: Vine leaf within inscription (year one of the redemption of Israel). AJC II, 265, 5.   650.00

137 138

137a. AE 23–25mm.
    O: Barbaric seven-branched palm tree with two bunches of dates; across field below, very crude and blundered inscription copying the legend of coin no. 137.
    R: Vine leaf surrounded by barbaric and retrograde inscription, copying coin no. 137. Spijkerman, Barbare 1, AJC II, 265, 5c.   800.00

138. AE 24.5mm.
    O: Seven-branched palm tree with two bunches of dates; across field below, inscription (Shma).
    R: Same as no. 137. AJC II, 270, 40.   750.00

139

139. AE 21–24mm.
    O: Palm branch upright within a wreath, surrounded by inscription (Simon Prince of Israel).
    R: Lyre of four (sometimes more) strings within inscription (year one of the redemption of Israel). AJC II, 265, 6.   750.00

140

140. AE 17.5mm.
    O: Seven-branched palm tree with two bunches of dates; across field below, inscription (Eleazar the priest).
    R: Bunch of grapes surrounded by inscription (year one of the redemption of Israel). AJC II, 265, 7.   350.00

A	B	C

A variety of this coin with a retrograde inscription on the obverse is frequently seen (AJC II-8). But the fabric of this variety is not crude at all and thus unlike most other coins with retrograde inscriptions. All four inscription varieties for this type are illustrated.

ירו שלם

שנת אחת לגאלת ישראל

141.   AE 19mm.
    O: Seven-branched palm tree with two bunches of dates; across field below, inscription (Jerusalem).
    R: Same as no. 140. AJC II, 265, 10.　　　　　　1,000.00

142　　　　　　143

Hybrid coins dated with both Year One and Year Two

142.　AR denarius, 3.26gm.
    O: Palm branch upright within inscription (year two of the freedom of Israel).
    R: Same as no. 140. AJC II, 268, 20.　　　　　　5,000.00

143.　AR denarius (pierced) 2.77gm.
    O: Three-stringed broad lyre within inscription (Year two of the freedom of Israel).
    R: Same as no. 140. AJC II, 267, 19.　　　　　　6,500.00

Coins of the Second Year (133–134 C.E.)

144.

144. AR tetradrachm, 14.17gm.
O: Facade of the Temple in Jerusalem with ark and scrolls (viewed from end) in center, inscription (Jerusalem) on sides, star above.
R: Lulav with etrog at left, surrounded by inscription (year two of the freedom of Israel). AJC II, 267, 13.   3,000.00

145. AR tetradrachm, 14.63gm.
O: Facade of the Temple in Jerusalem with ark and scrolls (viewed from end) in center, surrounded by inscription (Jerusalem).
R: Same as no. 144. AJC II, 266, 12.   8,500.00

146.

146. AR tetradrachm, 15.15gm.
O: Same as no. 144 except for the inscription, which is on the sides and reads (Shimon).
R: Same as no. 144 except for the style of the letter "shin." AJC II, 267, 16.   2,500.00

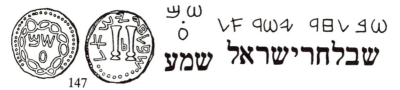

147.

147. AR denarius, 3.44gm.
O: Inscription within a wreath (Shim).
R: Two trumpets upright with inscription around and between (Year two of the freedom of Israel). AJC II, 268, 26.   650.00

148. AR denarius, 2.8gm.
      O: Same as no. 147.
      R: Jug with handle, palm branch at right, surrounded by inscription (year two of the freedom of Israel). AJC II, 268, 33.   500.00

149. AR denarius, 3.18gm.
      O: Same as no. 147.
      R: Palm branch upright with inscription around (year two of the freedom of Israel). AJC II, 268, 28.   500.00

150. AR denarius, 3.04gm.
      O: Inscription within a wreath (Shimon).
      R: Four-stringed elongated lyre, surrounded by inscription (year two of the freedom of Israel). AJC II, 268, 24.   600.00

148   151

151. AR denarius, 3.09gm.
      O: Same as no. 147.
      R: Three-stringed broad lyre, surrounded by inscription (year two of the freedom of Israel). AJC II, 268, 21.   1,250.00

152. AR denarius, 3.25gm.
      O: Bunch of grapes and small branch, inscription around lower half (Shimon).
      R: Three-stringed elongated lyre, surrounded by inscription (year two of the freedom of Israel). AJC II, 268, 25.   600.00

153. AR denarius, 3.41gm.
      O: Same as no. 152.
      R: Three-stringed broad lyre, surrounded by inscription (year two of the freedom of Israel). AJC II, 268, 23.   1,250.00

152   154

154. AR denarius, 3.20gm.
      O: Same as no. 152.
      R: Palm branch upright, surrounded by inscription (year two of the freedom of Israel). AJC II, 269, 31.   550.00

155

155. AR denarius, 2.86gm.
      O: Same as no. 152.
      R: Jug with handle, palm branch at right, surrounded by inscription
         (year two of the freedom of Israel). AJC II, 269, 36a.   500.00

156   157

156. AE 30.5mm.
      O: Inscription (Jerusalem) within a wreath.
      R: Amphora with two handles surrounded by inscription (year two
         of the freedom of Israel). AJC II, 269, 38.   5,500.00

157. AE 32mm.
      O: Inscription (Shimon) within a wreath.
      R: Amphora with two handles surrounded by inscription (year two
         of the freedom of Israel). AJC II, 270, 39.   6,500.00

158

158. AE 19/21mm.
      O: Upright palm branch within wreath, surrounded by inscription
         (Simon Prince of Israel).
      R: Four-stringed (or more) broad lyre surrounded by inscription
         (year two of the freedom of Israel). AJC II, 271, 46. 1,250.00

159   160

159.   AE 21.5mm.
       O: Upright palm branch within wreath, surrounded by inscription
          (for the freedom of Jerusalem).
       R: Four-stringed (or more) broad lyre surrounded by inscription
          (year two of the freedom of Israel). Similar coin to no. 158 but
          different obverse inscription. AJC II, 272, 50.   900.00

160.   AE 26mm.
       O: Seven-branched palm tree with two bunches of dates; across
          field below, inscription (Shim).
       R: Vine leaf within inscription (year two of the freedom of Israel).
          AJC II, 270, 43a.   250.00

160b   161

160a.   AE 22/24mm.
       (R:only). Similar coin except that a clear outline of the emperor's
       head (Vespasian?) to right is visible on the coin's reverse when
       it is viewed upside down.   250.00

160b.   AE 24.5mm.
       O: Seven-branched palm tree with two bunches of dates; across
          field below, inscription (Shimon).
       R: Vine leaf within inscription (year two of the freedom of Israel).
          BMC 44.   250.00
   Many interesting die varieties of this coin exist.

161.   AE 21.5mm.
       O: Seven-branched palm tree with two bunches of dates; across
          field below, inscription (Jerusalem).
       R: Bunch of grapes surrounded by inscription (Year two of the
          freedom of Israel). AJC II, 271, 49.   500.00

Undated Coins attributed to the Third Year (134–135 C.E.)

162.   AR tetradrachm, 13.36gm.
        O: Facade of the Temple in Jerusalem with ark and scrolls (viewed
            from end) in center, inscription on sides (Shimon) and star above.
        R: Lulav with etrog at left, surrounded by inscription (for the free-
            dom of Jerusalem). AJC II, 272, 51.   1,600.00

   A variety of this coin also occurs without the etrog (162a).

שמ **ענו**

לחרות ירושלם

163.   AR tetradrachm, 14.67gm.
        O: Facade of the Temple in Jerusalem with ark and scrolls (viewed
            from end) in center, inscription on sides (Shimon) and wavy
            line above.
        R: Lulav with etrog at left, surrounded by inscription (for the free-
            dom of Jerusalem). AJC II, 272, 53.   1,850.00

164.   AR denarius, 2.98gm.
        O: Inscription within a wreath (Shimon).
        R: Jug with handle, palm branch at right, surrounded by inscription
            (for the freedom of Jerusalem). AJC II, 274, 66.   375.00

   *The undated denarii of this series sometimes appear with an earlier form
of "Shimon" on the reverse, as on the coin no. 164b in the plates.*

164a. AR denarius, 3.08gm.
        O: Inscription within a wreath (Shimon).
        R: Jug with handle, surrounded by inscription (for the freedom of
            Jerusalem). AJC II, 275, 67.   400.00

165.   AR denarius, 3.46gm.
       O: Inscription within a wreath (Shimon).
       R: Two trumpets upright with pearl between, surrounded by in-
          scription (for the freedom of Jerusalem). AJC II, 273, 59b.
                                                                   425.00
166.   AR denarius, 2.97gm.
       O: Same as no. 164.
       R: Upright palm branch surrounded by inscription (for the freedom
          of Jerusalem). AJC II, 274, 62a.   375.00

167.   AR denarius, 3.30gm.
       O: Same as no. 164a.
       R: Three-stringed elongated lyre surrounded by inscription (for the
          freedom of Jerusalem). AJC II, 273, 55a.   375.00

168.   AR denarius, 3.01gm.
       O: Retrograde inscription within wreath (Shimon).
       R: Crude three-stringed elongated lyre with barbaric inscription
          (for the freedom of Jerusalem). AJC II, 273, 56b.   750.00

169.   AR denarius, 3.25gm.
       O: Bunch of grapes and small branch; inscription around lower half
          (Shimon).
       R: Upright palm branch surrounded by inscription (for the freedom
          of Jerusalem). AJC II, 274, 64.   375.00

170.   AR denarius, 3.03gm.
       O: Bunch of grapes and small branch; inscription around lower half
          (Shimon).
       R: Jug with handle, palm branch to right, surrounded by inscription
          (for the freedom of Jerusalem). AJC II, 275, 68.   375.00

171.   AR denarius, 3.15gm.
       O: Same as no. 169.
       R: Two trumpets upright with pearl between, surrounded by in-
          scription (for the freedom of Jerusalem). AJC II, 274, 60.
                                                                   400.00

172

173

172. AR denarius, 2.85gm.
      O: Same as no. 169.
      R: Three-stringed elongated lyre, surrounded by inscription (for
      the freedom of Jerusalem). AJC II, 273, 57b.   375.00

173. AE 26.5mm.
      O: Seven-branched palm tree with two bunches of dates; across
      field below, inscription (Shimon).
      R: Vine leaf within inscription (for the freedom of Jerusalem). AJC
      II, 278, 74.   250.00

174   176

174. AE 20.5mm.
      O: Three-stringed elongated lyre, inscription on sides (Shimon).
      R: Upright palm branch within wreath, surrounded by inscription
      (for the freedom of Jerusalem). AJC II, 276, 77.   250.00

175. AE 19mm.
      O: Seven-branched palm tree with two bunches of dates; across
      field below, inscription (Eleazar the priest).
      R: Bunch of grapes surrounded by inscription (for the freedom of
      Jerusalem). AJC II, 276, 79.   1,200.00

176. AE 17.5mm.
      O: Seven-branched palm tree with two bunches of dates; across
      field below, inscription (Jerusalem).
      R: Bunch of grapes surrounded by inscription (for the freedom of
      Jerusalem). AJC II, 276, 80.   250.00

177

177. AE 19mm.
       O: Seven-branched palm tree with two bunches of dates; across
       field below, inscription (Shimon).
       R: Bunch of grapes surrounded by inscription (for the freedom of
       Jerusalem). AJC II, 276, 81.   200.00

9. JUDAEA CAPTA AND RELATED ISSUES

Roman Republican Coins Relating to the Jews

Aristobulus was not able to make resistance, but was deserted in his first onset, and was driven to Jerusalem: he also had been taken at first by force, if Scarus, the Roman general, had not come and seasonably interposed himself and raised the siege. (Josephus, *Wars*, I, VI:2)

Roman Republic

178. AR denarius, 3.78gm.
 O: King Aretas kneels right with palm branch in left hand, next to camel; inscription above and below, M SCAUR AED CUR, EX SC across field.
 R: Jupiter drives quadriga left and hurls thunderbolts; inscription above PHYPSAE AEDCVR, on right CAPTVM, in ex. CHYPSAE COS PREIVE. Struck 58 B.C.E. Crawford 422.
                      125.00

This denarius, and another similar to it, was struck to commemorate the defeat by Pompey's general Marcus Scaurus of Aretas III, supporter of John Hyrcanus II in his battles against his brother, Judah Aristobulus II.

179

179. AR denarius, 3.91gm.
 O: Turreted bust of Cybelle right; surrounded by inscription A.PLAVTIVS AED.CVR.S.C.
 R: Bearded male figure kneels right with palm branch in left hand, next to camel; inscription BACCHIUS IVDAEVS. Struck 54 B.C.E. Crawford 431.   150.00

This coin is of the same reverse style as the previous one, with the exception of the inscription. The "Bacchius the Jew" referred to on this coin is one of the enigmas of Jewish numismatics. Narkiss said the coin represents Aristobulus II, commemorating his unsuccessful insurrection. Kindler, however, believes that the supplicant referred to is one Dionysius, ruler of Tripoli during this period.

Judaea Capta Coins

Thy men shall fall by the sword, And thy mighty in the war. And her gates shall lament and mourn; And utterly bereft she shall sit upon the ground. (Isaiah 3:25, 26)

So fell Jerusalem in the second year of Vespasian's reign, on the 8th September, captured five times before and now for the second time laid utterly waste. . . . There was no one left for the soldiers to kill or plunder. (Josephus, *The Jewish War*, 21, 22)

Coins, with all of their various functions in a society, were among the first efficient propaganda devices. Roman coins, notes historian Michael Grant, "served a propaganda purpose far greater than has any other national coinage before or since. This was the means which the Roman government, lacking modern media of publicity, used to insinuate into every house in the empire each changing nuance of imperial achievement and policy. Their unremitting use of this means is evidence enough . . . that in the course of their vast circulation these coins were studied with an attentiveness that is quite alien to our practices."

This description exactly defines the purpose of the extensive series of Judaea Capta coins issued under Vespasian and Titus following their victory against the Jews in 70 C.E. Even the third Flavian emperor, Domitian, issued a series of victory coins struck in Caesarea, although he had nothing to do with the campaigns against the Jews.

The Judaea Capta series was the broadest and most diverse series of coins commemorating a Roman victory issued in history to that time; hence it is clear that Vespasian and his sons fully intended for their victory over the Jews to be the "talk of the empire." Universal attention was their desire, observes H. St. J. Hart: "All the world must know and meditate the destruction of that rebellious and warlike nation, the Jews, and that a long and difficult war, with disturbing possibilities of complications throughout the empire is over."

No doubt Vespasian and his sons also looked at the victory as a stabilizing factor. It came, after all, just after Vespasian became emperor, after the alarming year of four emperors—Galba, Otho, Vitellius, and, finally, Vespasian himself.

Such a victory was the stuff of which a new dynasty was made, and Vespasian was successful in establishing it. What better way to let the world know of his strength, wisdom, and good judgement than to proclaim his greatest victory publically—even, perhaps, to make it sound more grandiose than it was.

Vespasian could proclaim his victory in a triumphal celebration, and by building a victory arch or two. But these were stationary items or single events—the people had to come to observe them. What was really needed was a form of mass communication to spread the word widely and often. The perfect vehicle for this was the coin of the realm, since coins were handled and examined many thousands of times each day throughout the empire.

Rome was the main mint for the coins of the Judaea Capta series, and they were issued in gold, silver, and bronze of all denominations. To further reinforce the idea of total victory over the Jewish nation, Judaea Capta coins were even issued locally in the Land of Israel, being struck in Caesarea and carrying Greek legends.

The Judaea Capta coins carry legends such as IVDAEA CAPTA, IVDAEA DEVICTA, and simply IVDAEA. Additionally, there are a number of VICTORIA AVGVSTI types that belong to this series. Some of the coins have no legend at all, the scene depicted telling the entire story.

The central device of virtually all of the Judaea Capta coins is a weeping Jewess; she usually sits mourning beneath a palm tree, the symbol of Judaea. Some of the coins also show a victorious emperor (or sometimes Nike in his place) dominating the scene, wearing battle dress, with sword and spear, foot resting on a helmet. Broken swords, shields, and other arms are sometimes scattered around the dejected mourner.

Coins of this series struck in the Land of Israel carry the legend ΙΟΥΔΑΙΑΣ ΕΑΛΩΚΥΙΑΣ, or "Judaea Vanquished."

The coins issued under Domitian from the Caesarea mint were included by a number of authors in the Judaea Capta series. This may or may not be the case. "No coin of Domitian bears a legend referring to such a victory [over the Jews], such as occurs on the coins of Vespasian and Titus," notes E. M. Weisbrem, who adds, "Domitian took no part in the war between Rome and Judaea and furthermore, as Titus' rival, tried to belittle his accomplishments. It is, therefore, most unlikely that Domitian would issue coins in commemoration of Titus' victory in Judaea."

Nevertheless, we observe that both Vespasian and Titus had succeeded in establishing themselves as strong emperors. Once Domitian had become emperor in his own right, and his brother and rival Titus was dead, he had nothing to lose by making subliminal connections with his renowned relatives. Thus it seems probable that the issuing of general victory-type coins from the Caesarea mint was meant as an imperial show of force harkening back to the dark days of a decade earlier, when Domitian's father and brother ravaged the Jewish nation and destroyed its spiritual hub. This Domitian, the coins warned, was not a man to be taken lightly.

Coins Commemorating Rome's Victory Over Judaea Struck in Palestine

180   181

180. AE 20mm.
   O: Laureate bust Vespasian right; inscription ΑΥΤΟΚΡ ΟΥΕΣΠ ΚΑΙΣΕΒ.
   R: Nike stands right with left foot on helmet; she writes with right hand on shield hanging from palm tree; surrounded by inscription ΙΟΥΔΑΙΑΣ ΕΑΛΩΚΥΙΑΣ. AJC II, Supp. VII, 1.
   650.00

181. AE 20 mm.
   O: Laureate bust Titus right; inscription ΑΥΤΟΚΡ ΤΙΤΟC ΚΑΙCΑP.
   R: Nike stands right with left foot on helmet; she writes with right hand on shield hanging from palm tree; surrounded by inscription ΙΟΥΔΑΙΑΣ ΕΑΛΩΚΥΙΑΣ. AJC II, Supp. VII, 2.
   250.00

182   183

182. AE 20mm.
   O: Laureate bust Titus right; inscription ΑΥΤΟΚΡ ΤΙΤΟC ΚΑΙΣΑΡ.
   R: Nike stands right, writing on shield supported by her knee, palm tree at right; surrounded by inscription ΙΟΥΔΑΙΑΣ ΕΑΛΩΚΥΙΑΣ. AJC II, Supp. VII, 3.   250.00

183. AE 24mm.
   O: Laureate bust Titus right; inscription ΑΥΤΟΚΡ ΤΙΤΟC ΚΑΙCΑP.
   R: Judaea sits mourning left below left of trophy, her hands tied behind her back, shield to right of trophy; inscription ΙΟΥΔΑΙΑΣ ΕΑΛΩΚΥΑΣ. AJC II, Supp. VII, 5.   350.00

Coins of Domitian Struck in Caesarea (81–96 C.E.)

184. AE 28mm.
O: Laureate bust Domitian right; inscription IMP CAES DOMIT AVG GERM PM TRP XI.
R: Seven-branched palm tree with two bunches of dates; surrounded by inscription IMP XXI COS XVI CENS P P P. AJC II, Supp. VIII, 9.   500.00

185. AE 23mm.
O: Laureate bust Domitian right; inscription IMP CAES DOMIT AVG GERM TR P XII.
R: Nike in flowing gown advances left, holding wreath in right hand and small trophy in left; surrounded by inscription IMP XXII COS XVI CENS PPP. AJC II, Supp. VIII, 10.   325.00

186. AE 16/18mm.
O: Laureate bust Domitian right; inscription IMP DOMITIANVS.
R: Nike in flowing gown advances left, holding wreath in right hand and trophy in left. AJC II, Supp. VIII, 8.   225.00

187. AE 28mm.
O: Laureate bust Domitian right; inscription DOMITIANVS CAES AVG GERMANICVS.
R: Minerva stands right on galley with shield in left hand and spear in right; on left is a trophy, on right a palm branch. AJC II, Supp. VIII, 6.   375.00

188. AE 23mm.
O: Laureate bust Domitian left; inscription DOMITIANVS CAES AVG GERMANICVS.
R: Minerva in flowing gown advances left holding trophy in right hand and shield and spear in left. AJC II, Supp. VIII, 7.   275.00

189. AE 20mm.
O: Laureate bust Domitian right; inscription IMP DOMIT AVG GERM.
R: Trophy surrounded by inscription VICTORIA AVG. AJC II, Supp. VIII, 5.   375.00

190.   AE 25mm.
    O: Laureate bust Domitian right; inscription DOMITIANVS
       CAESAR DIVI F AV.
    R: Nike in long gown advances left holding wreath in right hand,
       surrounded by inscription. VICTORIA AVG. AJC II, Supp.
       VIII, 3.   750.00

191.   AE 24mm.
    O: Laureate bust Domitian right; inscription IMP DOMI-
       TIANVS CAESAR DIVI F AV.
    R: Roman soldier faces front holding spear in right hand and an-
       other object in left; surrounded by inscription DIVOS AVG.
       AJC II, Supp. VIII, 2.   850.00

The Tenth Roman Legion

The reason for countermarking coins in ancient times has long been a subject of discussion among numismatists.

C. M. Kraay observed that "Conjectures upon the date and purpose of countermarks have been many and varied; to prolong the life of worn coins, to extend a restricted area of circulation, to meet some war-like emergency when normal supplies were interrupted, to proclaim revolt or to protest against the established government, to honor dead emperors or to complete the titulatures of living ones—all these theories, and more, have been championed and the truth must surely lie somewhere among them."

The coins countermarked by the Tenth Roman Legion, the *Legio Decima Fretensis*, are of special interest to the collector of ancient Jewish coins. The legion probably acquired its name *Fretensis* from the *Fretum Siculum*, the straits where the legion fought in the Sicilian War against Sextus Pompeius. Later the troops of the Tenth Legion were stationed in Syria.

They were ordered to help make up the forces that Vespasian led against Akko and other northern portions of the Land of Israel in his campaign of 66 C.E. The Tenth also made up a good part of the force that destroyed Jerusalem under Titus in 70 C.E. Three years later the same unit besieged and caused the destruction of the Zealot fortress of Massada.

The Tenth was made the permanent unit of the Roman province of Judaea. After the Bar Kochba War, the legion was garrisoned in Aelia Capitolina, while northern Israel was guarded by the Sixth Legion.

Insignias of the Tenth Legion were the boar and the galley, as well as various abbreviations of its name (LX, XF, LEX, and others). Dan Barag concludes that the coins countermarked by the Tenth Legion date from about 68 to 96 C.E. or 132 C.E. at the latest.

Countermarks of the Tenth Roman Legion

192.   COUNTERMARK: Within an incuse rectangle, L.X.F. above boar advancing right and dolphin below. Usually occurs with a second countermark of a galley to right within incuse rectangle.   400.00
193.   AE 13.5mm. Coin of Ascalon.
       O: Bust of Tyche with turreted crown right. Countermark LX within incuse rectangle.
       R: Galley right with A Σ above.   150.00
194.   AE 14mm. Coin of Ascalon.
       O: Bust of Tyche with turreted crown right. Countermark X with line above within incuse rectangle.
       R: Galley right inscription obliterated.   150.00
195.   AE 21.5. Titus.
       O: Bust right, very worn. Countermark of bust, possibly Nerva, right within incuse rectangle.
       R: Probably Judaea Capta type, but very worn. Countermark of galley right within incuse rectangle.   125.00
196.   AE 21/23mm. Coin of Caesarea under Nero.
       O: Laureate bust right, most of inscription obliterated. Countermark XF in incuse square.
       R: Tyche stands left holding bust in hand; inscription and date mostly obliterated. (See coin no. 241 for details of inscription and design.) Kadman 8, Barag plate IX, no. 6.   150.00
196a. The XF countermark appears on many of the coins struck in Antioch that date from before 66 C.E.   125.00

Vespasian (9–79 C.E.)

Titus Flavius Vespasianus was born in 9 C.E., the son of a tax collector and knight.

After serving as a legionary commander in the invasion of Britain (43–44 C.E.), consul and governor of Africa, and accompanying Nero to Greece in 66, Vespasian was sent to Judaea. His task was to suppress the Revolt of the Jews against their Roman overlords.

The Jews had already dealt some severe blows to Rome, but by June of the year 68 Vespasian had claimed victory over all of Judaea except Jerusalem and a few minor fortresses.

When Nero died, however, Rome was plunged into confusion, and three emperors followed in rapid succession.

In July 69, Vespasian's Eastern legions acclaimed him emperor. Shortly he returned to Rome and sent his son Titus to finish his chores in Judaea.

On June 23, 79, Vespasian died an apparently natural death.

The Judaea Capta coins of Vespasian were struck with many different obverse and reverse varieties. Only the general types are shown here.

Coins Depicting Vespasian Struck to Commemorate Victory Over the Jews

197. AU aureus.
      O: Laureate bust Vespasian right; surrounded by inscription, IMP
         CAESAR VESPASIANVS AVG.
      R: Jewess seated right mourning below right of trophy; in ex.
         IVDAEA. Struck 69–70. BMC 31.   6,000.00
198. AR denarius.
      O: Same as no. 197.
      R: Same as no. 197. RIC 15, Coh. 226.   375.00
199. AR denarius.
      O: Same as no. 197.
      R: Mourning Jewess seated right below palm tree, her hands are
         bound behind her; in ex. IVDAEA. RIC 16, Coh. 229.
                                                      550.00

200. AR denarius.
      O: Laureate bust Vespasian right; surrounded by inscription IMP
         CAESAR VESPASIANVS AVG TRP.
      R: Draped Jewess standing left with head bowed and hands tied to
         left of palm tree with fruit; inscription around IVDAEA DEV-
         ICTA. RIC 289, BMC 388.   850.00

200a. Plated denarius.
O: Laureate bust Vespasian right; surrounded by inscription IMP
    CAESAR VESPASIANVS AVG.
R: Same as no. 200. BMC 371, Coh. 242.   475.00

201

201. AE Sest.
O: Laureate bust Vespasian to right; inscription around, IMP
    CAES VESPASIAN AVG PM TRPPP COS III.
R: Jewess mourning seated right on right beneath palm tree; behind
    palm stands Jew with hands bound behind back, arms scattered
    around (the Jew is sometimes standing right and looking ahead;
    on other coins he stands left and looks back over his shoulder);
    inscription around IVDAEA CAPTA, in ex. SC. RIC 424–
    1, BMC 532 variety.   2,500.00

202. AE Sest.
O: Laureate undraped bust Vespasian right; inscription around,
    IMP CAES VESPASIAN AVG PM TRP PP COS III.
R: Jewess mourning seated left on left beneath palm tree; behind
    palm stands Jew, facing left, with hands tied behind back, arms
    scattered around; inscription around IVDAEA CAPTA, in
    ex. SC Coh. 238.   2,750.00

203

203. AE Sest.
O: Laureate bust Vespasian to right; inscription around, IMP
    CAES VESPASIAN AVG PM TR PPP COS III.
R: Jewess mourning sits right on right beneath palm tree, behind
    palm stands the emperor with spear and parazonium; inscription
    IVDAEA CAPTA, in ex. SC. RIC 427–1, Coh. 239.
                                                         2,500.00

204.

204. AE Sest.
O: Laureate bust Vespasian left, IMP CAES VESPASIAN
AVG PM TR PPP COS III.
R: Jewess mourning sits right on right beneath palm tree; behind
palm stands Victory with foot on helmet, set to write on shield;
inscription around, VICTORIA A V GVSTI, in ex. SC.
RIC 468–3, BMC 785.   1,250.00

205. AE dupondius.
O: Radiate bust Vespasian right, globe below his neck; inscription
IMP CAESAR VESPASIAN AVG COS III.
R: Draped Victory advances right on ship's prow, holding wreath
in right hand and palm branch over shoulder in left; inscription
VICTORIA NAVALIS, across field SC. BMC 809, C
633.   250.00

*It is doubtful that this coin commemorates the naval victory of the Romans
over the Jews on the Sea of Galilee during the First Revolt. However, this
tale persists, and even though the coin is as likely to commemorate Roman
victories other than those in Judaea, it is included.*

206.   207.

206. AR denarius.
O: Laureate bust Vespasian right; inscription IMP CAES VESP
AVG PM COS IIII.
R: Jewess mourning sits right on right below palm tree; behind
palm stands the emperor with spear and parazonium; no in-
scription. BMC 511.   850.00

207. AR denarius.
O: Laureate bust Vespasian right; inscription IMP CAES VESP
AVG PM COS IIII.
R: Victory advances to right holding branch over shoulder with left
hand; right hand places wreath on a legionary standard at right;
inscription VICTORIA AVGVSTI. RIC 52, BMC 75.
225.00

208. AE Sest.
O: Laureate draped bust Vespasian right; inscription around, IMP
CAES VESPAS AVG PM TRP PP COS IIII.
R: Jew stands left on right beneath palm tree, his hands bound
behind him; on left of palm, facing right stands the emperor
with spear and parazonium; inscription IVDAEA CAPTA,
in ex. SC. H. Cahn, Num. Chr. 1946, Pl. 1–5. EXT. RARE

209. AE as.
O: Lauratebust Vespasian left; inscription outwards, IMP CAE-
SAR VESPASIAN COS VIII.
R: Draped Victory stands right on ship's prow, holding up a wreath
in right hand and in left a palm branch over her shoulder; inscription VICTORIA AVGVST, across field SC. BMC
740, RIC 600.   200.00

210

210. AE as.
O: Laureate bust Vespasian right; inscription IMP CAES VES-
PASIAN AVG COS VIII PP.
R: Jewess mourning sits right on right below palm tree; arms scat-
tered around; inscription IVDAEA CAPTA, in ex. SC.
RIC 762, BMC 845.   650.00

211   212

211. AR denarius.
O: Laureate bust Vespasian right; inscription outward, IMP
CAESAR VESPASIANVS AVG.
R: Victory advancing left erecting a trophy; beneath it sits weeping
Jewish captive to left; inscription TR POT X COS VIIII.
Struck 79 C.E. BMC 246. RIC 114.   275.00

212. AR denarius.
O: Laureate bust Vespasian right; inscription DIVVS AV-
GVSTVS VESPASIANVS.
R: Draped Victory strides left with both hands placing round shield
on a trophy; a mourning Jewess sits left below; across field EX.
SC. BMC 112 (Titus).   275.00

Titus (39–81 C.E.)

Titus Flavius Vespasianus succeeded his father on the throne immediately upon his death in 79 C.E.

When Vespasian returned to Rome from Judaea he entrusted the Jewish War to his eldest son. Titus was victorious in 70 C.E.

Titus was in love with the Jewish princess Julia Berenice, sister of Agrippa II. They lived together in Rome for a while, but he soon sent her away. She returned when he became emperor, but he rejected her again. It is said that Titus was truly in love with Berenice, but couldn't risk the wrath he would incur by marrying a Jewish princess.

Titus died an apparently natural death at age 42, on September 13, 81. He was succeeded by his younger brother Domitian.

The Judaea Capta coins of Titus were struck with many different obverse and reverse varieties. Only the general types are shown here.

Coins Depicting Titus Struck to Commemorate Victory Over the Jews

213

213.   AR denarius.
    O: Laureate bust Titus right; inscription around, T CAESAR IMP VESPASIANVS.
    R: Captive kneels right in front of trophy, hands are bound behind back. Trophy is made of helmet, cuirass, crossed swords and shield; inscription around TR POT VII COS VII. Struck 79 C.E. RIC 208 (Vesp.), BMC 258 (Vesp.).   375.00

214

214.   AR denarius.
    O: Laureate, draped bust Titus right; inscription T CAES IMP VESP PON TR POT.
    R: Titus laureate standing in triumphal quadriga right, holding branch in right hand and sceptre in left; no inscription. Struck 72–73 C.E. BMC 521 (Vesp.).   350.00

The reverse of this coin shows a scene identical to one shown on the arch of Titus, commemorating the victory over the Jews.

214a. AE sestertius.
O: Laureate, bearded head of Titus to right, T CAES VESPA-
SIAN IMP PON TR POT COS II.
R: Emperor holding branch and sceptre, stands in triumphal quad-
riga pacing to right, SC in exergue. BMC (Vesp.) 141.636.
2,500.00

215. AR denarius, 3.22gm.
O: Laureate, bearded bust Titus right; inscription IMP TITVS
CAES VESPASIAN AVG P M.
R: Two captives (naked man on right, draped woman on left) seated
back to back; between them is a trophy made of helmet, cuirass
and oblong shields; inscription TR P IX IMP XV COS
VIII PP. RIC 21a, BMC 37. Struck 80 C.E.   850.00

216. AE Sestertius.
O: Laureate bust Titus right (or left); inscription IMP T CAES
VESP AVG PM TR PPP COS VIII.
R: Jewess mourning sits left on left of palm tree on pile of arms;
on other side of tree mourning Jew with hands bound looks back
over shoulder (or faces right), helmet and yoke on ground;
across field IVD CAP SC in ex (or across field). BMC 169
variety, RIC 91.   3,250.00

216a. AE sestertius.
O: Similar to 214a.
R: Victory stands right, with left foot on helmet, she inscribes a
shield set on palm tree, VICTORIA AVGVSTI SC. BMC
(Vesp.) 141.638.   2,250.00

217. AE as.
O: Laureate bust Titus right; inscription T CAES IMP PON
TRP COS II CENS.
R: Jewess mourning sits right on right below palm tree, arms scat-
tered around; inscription IVDAEA CAPTA, in ex. SC.
RIC 653, BMC 672.   750.00
218. AE semis.
O: Laureate head Titus right; inscription around, IMP T CAE-
SAR DIVI VESPASI AVG.
R: Mourning Jewess sits left on left below palm tree, arms and yoke
scattered about; inscription across field, IVD CAP SC. RIC
141, BMC 259.   EXT. RARE

The Coin of Nerva, 96 to 98 C.E.

Domitian was a cruel and vindictive man, who continued to collect the
Jewish Tax his father had imposed upon all Jews in the Roman Empire.
The tax was two drachmas, half a shekel, since Vespasian had reasoned
that the Jews could enrich his coffers instead of offering the tribute they
had voluntarily paid to their own Temple, as prescribed in Exodus 30:13.
    Domitian ordered his tax collectors to work with a vengeance never
imagined by his father and brother. Collectors often applied severe insult
and abuse (*calumnia*) during their collection. To collect the tax from a
Jew, first of all, they had to determine whether the man was indeed a Jew.
The fastest way of doing this was to see if he had been circumcised. Thus
the unscrupulous tax collectors frequently demanded humiliating exposure
of the genitals, usually in public places or official meetings, but also at
family gatherings or other times when embarrassment would be caused.
    According to the Roman historian Seutonius: "More than any other,
the FISCUS JUDAICUS was administered very severely; and to it were
brought, or reported, those who either had lived the life of a Jew unpro-
fessed, or concealing their origin, had not paid the tax imposed upon the
people. I remember that it was of interest to me during my youth when a
ninety-year-old man was brought before the procurator and a very crowded
court to see whether he was circumcised."

When Domitian was assassinated on September 18, 96 C.E., Nerva succeeded him. Nerva instituted an extensive series of popular changes, one of which was the abolition of the insulting method of collecting the Jewish Tax. The tax itself was not revoked, only the degrading method of collecting it. To proclaim his benevolence, Nerva ordered this coin to be issued.

Incidentally, the Jewish Tax apparently remained in effect until the reign of Julian the Apostate, 361–363 C.E. In a letter to the Jews, he says: "In the past your liability to new taxes and the constraint to give to the treasury numberless quantities of gold made the yoke of servitude especially oppressive. With my own eyes I have seen a part of this misery; a larger one I have perceived by finding the rolls kept to be used against you. I have reduced these rolls to ashes."

 219

Nerva

219. AE Sest.
      O: Laureate bust Nerva right; inscription, IMP NERVA CAES AVG PM TRP COS III PP.
      R: Large palm tree with two bunches of dates, surrounded by inscription FISCI IVDAICI CALVMNIA SVBLATA (the insult of the Jewish Tax has been removed), across field large SC. Struck Rome 97 C.E. RIC 82.   4,500.00

Coins of Hadrian, 117 to 138 C.E.

Hadrian traveled across his entire empire during his reign. In 130 C.E. he traveled from Arabia to Egypt by way of Judaea. On these journeys the emperor secured his borders and instituted necessary government offices. Hadrian had coins issued to commemorate his visits to various provinces, including Egypt, Macedonia, and Spain, as well as Judaea. It is not known whether these coins were issued to commemorate Hadrian's victory over Bar Kochba, or prior to the outbreak of hostilities.

Hadrian

220. AE Sest.
O: Bareheaded bust right; surrounded by inscription, HAD-
RIANVS AVG. COS.III.PP.
R: Hadrian stands to right raising right hand facing Judaea, who
holds a box and a patera over altar, Judaea is flanked by two
children facing left and holding palm branches, a bull stands
behind the altar; surrounded by inscription. ADVENTVI.
AVG. IVDAEAE, in ex. SC. RIC 890.   6,000.00

221. AE Sest.
O: Bareheaded bust right; surrounded by inscription, HAD-
RIANVS AVG. COS.III.P.P.
R: Hadrian stands to right raising right hand, facing Judaea, who
holds a patera over altar and a box, an altar and a sacrificial
bull stand between the two, a child stands on left of Judaea and
two children holding palms advance toward Hadrian; in ex.
IVDAEA, in field left and right, SC. RIC 853.
EXT. RARE

10. CITY COINS OF ANCIENT ISRAEL AND TRANSJORDAN

Even before the first Hasmonean coins were struck, a few important cities in ancient Israel issued their own coins. But the vast majority of city coins were issued after Augustus, when Roman authorities gave minting privileges to certain cities. Such powers were granted to promote both loyalty to Rome and commerce in the area.

Most of the city coins were issued between the late first century and the middle third century C.E. Although coins were minted in several cities of ancient Israel prior to the first century, these were either major official coins or provincial coins and not local issues. Thus even if they were struck in specific cities, they are not usually referred to as city coins *per se*.

The city coins circulated in ancient Israel together with other coins of the area. City coinage came to an end about 260 C.E. when the economy changed so much that the value of the bronze was greater than the nominal value of the coins.

Most city coins of ancient Israel carry Greek rather than Latin inscriptions, evidence that Greek was still spoken in the area at this time. Frequently, the city coins bear the portraits of the emperors under whom they were issued. However, the coins are not dated by regnal years, but mainly according to eras of each individual city.

The series of city coins of ancient Israel can be read as history books. Referring to the large number of coins struck by the cities of the Roman Empire, M. Rostovtzeff observed that they "supply us with first-class information on some important points in their political, religious and economic life. These sources have revealed to us not only the external appearance of many ancient cities but also the main features of every aspect of their life—their walls, streets, gates, public places, public and private buildings, on the one hand, and on the other their municipal organization, their income and expenditure, their wealth and their sources of wealth, both public and private, their religious beliefs, their amusements and their intellectual interests."

The study of the city coins of ancient Israel has only just begun to come into its own. After the establishment of the State of Israel in 1948, the first numismatic boom was the study of the ancient Jewish coin issues. While interest in those coins remains high, it is really only in the last several years that a large number of Jewish numismatists have begun to look carefully at the city coins; hence many discoveries remain to be made in this field.

Panias (Caesarea Philippi, Baniyas)

When Jesus came into the coasts of Caesarea Philippi, he asked his disciples, saying, "whom do men say that I, the Son of Man, am?" (Matthew 16:13)

Panias, modern Baniyas, is located by the freshwater springs that flow from the mountains into the Sea of Galilee. Here local folk worshipped the flute-playing god Pan, and even today niches where statues of Pan once stood can be seen carved into the hillsides.

A temple to Augustus was built here by Herod I. Later Herod Philip II built up the city as his capital and named it Caesarea Philippi in honor of Augustus.

Agrippa II also used the city as his capital but renamed it Neronias in honor of his own patron, Nero.

Earlier in history, near Panias, Antiochus III defeated the Ptolemaic general Scopas in 198 B.C.E. In good part because of this battle, Egypt surrendered its territories in the Land of Israel, which then fell under control of the Seleucids.

The coins of Panias were issued from the time of Augustus (27 B.C.E.–14 C.E.) through the reign of Elagabalus (218–222 C.E.). Many of the coins of Panias show Pan playing his pipes, or the pipes alone on some of the smaller denominations. The era of Panias began in 4 B.C.E.

Panias

222

222. AE 13mm.
   O: Undraped, beardless bust of ? to right.
   R: Syrinx (pipes) surrounded by inscription, KAICAP ΠΑΝ-ΙΑΔΟC, POB (of Caesarea Panias, 172). Struck 169–170 C.E. Ros 14.   350.00

223

223. AE 25mm. Marcus Aurelius.
   O: Laureate, draped bust right, inscription around, AYT KAICM AYP ANTWNEINOC CEB.
   R: Nude Pan stands front leaning against tree with legs crossed, playing a flute, surrounded by inscription KAIC CEB IEP KAI ACY T ΠΠΑΝΙW, POB (of Caesarea, Augustan, holy city of asylum at Panias, 172). Struck 169 C.E. Ros 18.   500.00

Akko (Ptolemais, Acre)

Asher drove not out the inhabitants of Acco.   (Judges 1:31)

The city which is known today as Acre forms the northern tip of the Bay of Haifa. It has been in continuous existence for more than 3,000 years, having been mentioned in an inscription of Tuthmosis III from 1479 B.C.E.

Describing Akko, Josephus wrote, "It is a maritime city, situated in a great plain but surrounded by mountains." The city was the terminus of a famous trade route of the ancient world.

In the third century B.C.E. Alexander the Great established a very active mint of gold, silver, and bronze coins here. The city received the name Ptolemais when it was taken from Seleucus by Ptolemy II of Egypt about 221 B.C.E. In 200 B.C.E. it fell back into the hands of the Seleucids when it was captured by Antiochus III (the Great).

Ptolemais with other coastal cities, was constantly hostile to the Jewish cause during the Maccabean wars. In 104 B.C.E. Alexander Jannaeus besieged Ptolemais, but he was unable to capture the city. This rebuff proved a turning point for Jannaeus, who never again tried to extend the rule of his kingdom farther to the north.

In 40 B.C.E., as they marched into Judaea allied with Mattathias Antigonus, the Parthians scared Herod I out of Ptolemais. Herod had revenge, however, for when he returned from Rome to regain his crown he landed in Ptolemais and the Parthians had to withdraw.

When Herod was changing his loyalties from Mark Antony to Octavian, he greeted the future Augustus as he arrived in Ptolemais in 30 B.C.E.

The city served as a residence for the Roman governors of Syria when they came from Antioch to see to matters of Judaea, and it was also the main operational base for Roman forces during activity in the north. Vespasian headquartered his troops here in 67 C.E. when he moved against the forces of Josephus in Galilee.

Akko's first coins were issued under the Ptolemaic Dynasty, and coins were issued here until the death of Gallienus in 268 C.E. The coins of Akko carry such symbols as the club, caduceus, and thunderbolt. Temples and shrines as well as the personages of Tyche, Sarapis, Aphrodite, and others also appear on the coins. Ptolemaic and Seleucid coins were also minted here. The local era dates from 48 B.C.E.

Akko

224. AE 15mm.
   O: Laureate head Zeus right.
   R: Upside down club within wreath, Greek inscription on either side, COL PTOL. Kad. 91, Ros. 45.   175.00

225. AE 24mm. Nero.
O: Laureate head right, Latin inscription around, IMP.NER.CLA.CAES.AVG.GER.P.M.TR.P.
R: Founder ploughs to right with cow and ox, rising from behind are four standards inscribed III, V, X, XII. Between the standards, C O L CL A PTOL; around, DIVOS CLAVD STAB GER FELIX. Kad. 92.   250.00

226. AE 23mm. Trajan.
O: Laureate, undraped bust right; inscription around, IMP CAES NER TRAIANO OPT AVG GERM.
R: Tyche seated to right on rock, holding ears of corn in right hand, river god below; inscription around COL PTOL. Kad. 97, Ros. 47.   175.00

227. AE 19mm. Hadrian.
O: Laureate, draped bust to right, inscription around, IMP TRA HADRIANO CAESARI.
R: Rev. Tyche stands left wearing kalathos, holding rudder in right hand, cornucopia in left; inscription, COL PTOL. Ros. 49. Kad. 107.   175.00

228. AE 26mm. Valerian.
O: Laureate, draped bust to right; inscription around, IMP C P LIC VALERIANVS AVG.
R: Sacred tree flanked by two altars, a serpent arising from each; caduceus to right; inscription, COL PTOL. Kad. 246, Ros. 82.   350.00

Tiberias (Tveriah)

Howbeit there came other boats from Tiberias nigh unto the place where they did eat bread, after that the Lord had given thanks.   (John 6:23)

On the western shore of the Sea of Galilee lies Tiberias. Herod Antipas founded the city in 18 C.E. (beginning the local era) and moved his captital here from Sepphoris, precipitating a long political rivalry between the two cities.

After the death of Agrippa I, Tiberias was ruled by the Roman procurators. The city remained Galilee's capital until 61 C.E., when Nero gave Tiberias to Agrippa II.

Josephus reports that at first Jews were reluctant to settle in this city, since a burial ground was uncovered as the city was being built. Antipas solved the problem by populating Tiberias with poor, landless men, freedmen, and soldiers, in addition to wealthy families with no strong religious commitments.

Tiberias was laid out like a Roman city. It was adorned with public buildings, a large synagogue, a stadium, and a palace.

After the Bar Kochba War the city was paganized by Hadrian, but soon it became a major Jewish religious center when Johanan ben Nappaph settled there early in the third century C.E. Tiberias was the last city in which the Sanhedrin sat.

It was in Tiberias that Rabbi Yehudah Hanassi made the final revision of the Mishna. Two hundred years later the Jerusalem Talmud took its final shape here. The Talmud and the Mishna refer to 13 synagogues in Tiberias. Rabbi Yehochanan ben Zakkai and Rabbi Akiba are among the famous rabbis buried in this city.

Tiberias is built upon a number of hot springs which in ancient times— and even today—were believed to have special medicinal value. Some of the city's coins are decorated with Hygeia, goddess of health, in a reference to these springs.

The first coins of Tiberias were issued during the reign of Claudius in 53 C.E. and the last in the time of Elagabalus in 222 C.E. Zeus, Sarapis, Poseidon, Tyche, and Nike are a few of the other gods and goddesses who adorn the coins of Tiberias. The coins of Herod Antipas were struck here, and most of them carry the city's name.

229

Tiberias

229. AE 24mm. Trajan.
   O: Undraped, laureate bust to right; inscription around, AYTKAI
   NEP TPAIANOC CEB ΓEP.
   R: Hygeia wearing long dress sits right on rock, holds serpent in
   right hand and feeds it with her left: surrounded by inscription
   TIBEPI KΛAYΔI, and date across field ET AΠ. Struck
   99–100 C.E. BMC 10, Ros. 6.   225.00

230

231

230. AE 27mm. Trajan.
   O: Laureate bust to right; inscription around, AYTOKP KAIC
   NEP TPAIANOC CEB ΓEPM.
   R: Tyche wearing long gown stands left, holding rudder in right
   hand, cornucopia in left, prow to left at her feet; surrounded by
   inscription TIBEPIEW NKΛAYΔIO, ET AΠ (of the peo-
   ple of Tiberias Claudia, year 81). Struck 99–100 C.E. BMC 7,
   Ros. 5.   225.00

231. AE 19mm. Trajan.
   O: Laureate, undraped bust to right; inscription around, AYT
   KA NE TPAIANOC CE ΓEP.
   R: Two crossed cornucopiae with palm branch between; surrounded
   above by inscription TIBEP KAΛYΔ, date in field, E T
   ȳ. Struck 99–100 C.E. BMC 17 variety, Ros. 9.   225.00

232

233

232. AE 23mm. Hadrian.
   O: Laureate bust to right wearing paludamentum and cuirass; inscription around, AYT TPA AΔPIANW KAIC CEB.
   R: Zeus seated left, holding sceptre in left hand, within four-col-
   umned temple; surrounded by inscription TIBEP KΛAYΔ,
   date in exergue, ET AP. Struck 119–120 C.E. BMC 24, Ros.
   12.   225.00

233. AE 19mm. Hadrian.
O: Laureate, draped bust to right; inscription around, AYT AΔ-
PIANW KAIC CEB.
R: Winged Nike to front, wearing long gown, head left, she advances right holding wreath in right hand and palm branch in
left; surrounded by inscription, TIBEP KΛAYΔ, date
across field LAP. Struck 119–120 c.e. BMC 32–33, Ros.
14.   200.00

Sepphoris (Diocaesarea, Zippori)

*All whose fathers are known to have held office as public officers or
almoners may marry into the Priestly stock and none need trace their
descent. R. Jose says: Also any whose name was signed as a witness in the
old archives at Sepphoris. (Mishnah, Kiddushin, 4:5)*

Sepphoris (Diocaesarea) is known today as Zippori and lies some four
miles northwest of Nazareth. When Pompey conquered the Land of Israel
in 64 B.C.E. Sepphoris became a capital.

Herod I conquered the city near the beginning of his reign, in a battle
that took place during a snowstorm. Sepphoris was inherited by Herod
Antipas after his father died. Antipas rebuilt and fortified the city and
made it capital of Galilee, a position it held until Tiberias was
founded.

During early Roman times the city was largely populated by non-Jews,
and it remained on the Roman side during the First Revolt. Sepphoris
later became a key center of Jewish learning, however, and it was for some
time the seat of the Sanhedrin.

The city was probably renamed Diocaesarea by Hadrian. The prefix
"Dio" stands for Zeus. A temple dedicated to Jupiter, Juno, and Minerva
was also dedicated here by Hadrian, who enlarged the city considerably.

The earliest coins of Sepphoris were issued in 68 c.e. by Vespasian under
the emperor Nero, and establish that Vespasian was a governor as well as
a general before he took the throne. The latest of this city's coins come
from the time of Elagabalus (218–222 c.e.). Because of the importance
of the Jewish community in Sepphoris, most of its coins do not offend
religious feelings; they carry wreaths, cornucopiae, and palm trees. Later
coins were struck with pagan temple motifs.

236

Sepphoris

234. AE 24mm. Nero.
O: Two cornucopiae crossed, caduceus arising between them; inscription around, ΕΠΙ ΟΥΕΣΠΑΣΙΑΝΟΥ ΕΡΗΝΟΠΟΛΙ ΝΕΡWΝΙΑ ΣΕΠφW.
R: Inscription and date surrounded by wreath, LΔΙ/ΝΕΡΩΝΟ/ΚΛΑΥΔΙΟΥ/ΚΑΙСΑΡΟ/С (Year 14). Struck 67/68 c.e. BMC page 239 no. 5, Ros. 1.   750.00

235. AE 27mm. Trajan.
O: Undraped laureate bust to right; inscription around, ΤΡΑΙΑΝΟΣ ΑΥΤΟΚΡΑΤΩΡ ΕΔΩΚΕΝ.
R: Inscription surrounded by a wreath, ΣΕΠφΩ ΡΗΝΩΝ (of the people of Sepphoris). BMC 1, Ros. 3.   225.00

234   235

236. AE 22mm. Trajan.
O: Laureate undraped bust to right; inscription around, ΤΡΑΙΑΝΟΣ ΑΥΤΟΚΡΑΤΩΡ ΕΔΩΚΕΝ.
R: Eight-branched palm tree bearing two bunches of dates; inscription across field, ΣΕΠφΩΡΗΝΩΝ. BMC 5, Ros. 4.   200.00

237   238

237. AE 20mm. Trajan.
O: Laureate undraped bust to right; inscription around, ΤΡΑΙΑΝΟΣ ΑΥΤΟΚΡΑΤΩΡ ΕΔΩΚΕΝ
R: Large caduceus tied with bow; inscription ΣΕΠφΩΡΗΝΩΝ. BMC 14, Ros. 5.   225.00

238. AE 23mm. Antoninus Pius.
O: Laureate bust right wearing paludamentum; inscription around,
AYT KAI ANTWNINW CEBEYC.
R: Tyche stands right within center arch of tetrastyle temple, she
wears turreted crown and long dress, right hand on sceptre and
left holds cornucopia; inscription begins in exergue and reads
outward, ΔIOKAI IEPA ACY AYTO (of the people of
Diocaesarea, holy city of asylum, autonomous). BMC 21.

275.00

Dora (Dor, Tantura)

The son of Abinadab, in all the region of Dor.   (1 Kings 4:11)

Dora, as Naphoth-dor, was an important Royal Canaanite city in the League of Jabin, the king of Hazor.

In the 12th century B.C.E. it fell into the hands of the Philistines. Dora became a colony of Sidon in the Persian period and during the early Hellenistic period it was a royal fortress of the Ptolemies.

At the end of the second century B.C.E., Dora was in the hands of Zoilus, a tyrant who also ruled Strato's Tower (later Caesarea).

Dora was outside the limits of the Biblical Land of Israel until it was annexed by Alexander Jannaeus, who acquired it not by war but through negotiation. Pompey later conquered the city and returned it to its former owners. Dora apparently remained free under the Herodian rulers until it was annexed to the province of Phoenicia in the second century C.E.

Dora is associated with the modern Dor, on the Mediterranean Coast some 18 miles south of Haifa.

The first coins of Dora were issued in 63 B.C.E. and continued until the reign of Caracalla (198–217 C.E.). Symbolized on the coins of Dora are Doros, the city's legendary founder, the city goddess Tyche, and other figures and designs, including the galley. The era of Dora is dated from 63 B.C.E.

Dora

239.   AE 22mm.
    O: Laureate bust Doros right.
    R: Astarte moving to left wearing turreted crown and long chiton,
    holding standard in right hand and cornucopia in left; inscription,
    ΔWPIETWN,   (of the people of Dora, 131). Struck 67–68 C.E.
    Ros. 19, BMC 8.   275.00
240.   AE 27mm. Trajan.
    O: Laureate, draped bust right, star in front; inscription around,
    AVTOK KAIC NEP TPAIANOC CEB ΓEPM . . .
    R: Laureate bust Doros right, aphlaston in front: inscription
    around, ΔWP IEP ACYΛ AYTON NAYAP, (holy Dora,
    city of asylum, autonomous, ruler of the seas, 175). Struck 111–
    112 C.E. Ros. 26 BMC 30.   325.00

Gaba

Little is known about the ancient city of Gaba. Indeed, it was only recently
ascertained that the most probable location of ancient Gaba is in the Jezreel
Valley, on a hill next to Kibbutz Mishmar Ha'emek.

    The city was founded by Gabinius, and possibly its name is linked to
him. Some of the coins carry the legend "Gaba, named after Philip and
Claudius," and it is possible that the Philip named is either Herod Philip
II or a legendary Philip such as Philip of Macedon.

Gaba   240a

240a. AE 18mm. Sabina.
    O: Bust of Sabina to right; inscription, CABINA CEBACTH.
    R: Men stands to front, holding spear and sword; inscription, KΛ
    ΦI ΓABHNWN ZOP (Claudia Philippi Gaba, 177). Ros. 13.
    Struck 117 C.E. $400.00

Caesarea (Strato's Tower)

*Which when the brethren knew, they brought him down to Caesarea and
sent him forth to Tarsus.* (Acts 9:30)

Caesarea was founded in 12 C.E. by Herod I on the decaying remains of
a Phoenician town called Strato's Tower. Herod named the city after the

emperor Augustus Caesar, and built a temple to him here, as well as a great harbor city.

Upon Herod's death the city was passed along to his son Archelaus, but when Archelaus was banished Caesarea became the seat of the Roman Procurators of Judaea. This it remained except for a brief period (41–44 C.E.) when it was ruled by Agrippa I.

Vespasian held a special fondness for Caesarea, since it was here that his troops had proclaimed him emperor. As a token of his gratitude he gave the city the rank of a Roman Colony with limited rights and renamed it "Colonia Prima Flavia Caesarea" or "The First Flavian Imperial Colony, Caesarea."

The first coins of Caesarea were minted under Claudius (41–54 C.E.) and the last ones during the reign of Volusianus in 253 C.E. The coins of Caesarea carry depictions of Tyche, the city goddess, Sarapis, Dionysus, and Demeter. A numerically large series shows an eagle supporting the letters SPQR for "The Senate and the Roman People."

Caesarea

241. AE 21mm. Nero.
O: Laureate undraped bust right; inscription around, ΣΕΒΑΣΤΟΣ NEPWN ΚΑΙΣΑΡ.
R: Tyche wearing turreted crown and short gown stands left, right foot on prow, cross-headed standard in left hand, a human bust in right; date in left field, LIΔ; inscription around, ΣΕ-ΒΑΣΤW ΛΙΜΕΝΙ ΚΑΙΣΑΡΙΑ ΠΡΟΣ. BMC 23 variety Kad. 1.   250.00
242. AE 26mm. Trajan.
O: Laureate undraped bust right; inscription around, IMP CAES NER TRAIANO OP AVG GER DA COS VI PP.
R: Emperor standing and holding cornucopia, sacrificing at altar on left; inscription around, COL. PRI FL. AVG. CAESAR-ENS. BMC 42, Kad. 23, Ros. 20.   250.00
243. AE 20mm. Hadrian.
O: Draped laureate bust right; inscription around, IMP TRA HADRIANO CAES AVG.
R: Apollo standing left holding snake, beside him on right a sacrificial tripod; inscription, CIF AVG CAESAR. Kad. 29, Ros. 25.   225.00

244.   AE 22mm. Severus Alexander.
       O: Laureate undraped bust to right; inscription around, IMPCAE
       SEV ALEXANDER.
       R: Eagle supporting wreath containing SPQR on spread wings; in-
       scription around, C I F A FC CAE METROPO. BMC
       126, Kad. 97.   200.00

245.   AE 27mm. Trajan Decius.
       O: Laureate bust right wearing paludamentum and cuirass; inscrip-
       tion around, IMP C G MES Q TRA DECIVS AVG.
       R: Horned altar with two trees rising above from behind; inscription
       around, COL PR F AVG FC CAES METRP. BMC
       159, Kad. 154, Ros. 129.   375.00

246.   AE 21mm. Hostilian.
       O: Laureate bust right, wearing paludamentum and cuirass; inscrip-
       tion around, HOSTILIANO QVINTOC.
       R: Bust of Tyche right, wearing turreted crown with partly bared
       bust; inscription around, COL P F AV FC CAES
       METRO. BMC 191, Kad. 187, Ros. 154   350.00

Nysa-Scythopolis (Bet-Shean, Beisan)

*And they put his armour in the house of the Ashtaroth; and they fastened
his body to the wall of Beth-shan.*   (I Samuel 31:10)

Nysa-Scythopolis is the ancient Bet Shean, the modern Beisan. The city
was first mentioned in the Tell El Amarna letters nearly 3,500 years ago.
It has been a strategic city from ancient times, for it lies on key caravan

routes that linked Egypt and Mesopotamia. In fact, the city is known as the key to Western Palestine.

It was in Bet Shean that the Philistines displayed the body of King Saul after he was defeated and fell upon his own sword to avoid capture. King David later retook the city in reprisal. In about 700 B.C.E. the site was apparently deserted and was not reoccupied until Hellenistic times, when it was renamed Scythopolis, "City of the Scythians."

The city received the Nysa portion of its name in the second century B.C.E. under the Seleucids, who were commemorating the nurse of Dionysus who had been born there, according to legends.

John Hyrcanus I captured Nysa and in 63 B.C.E. it was taken by Pompey and made the capital city of the Roman Decapolis. Nysa's local era begins with this occasion. It was the only city of the Decapolis lying west of the Jordan River.

Coins were minted under the city's authority from 40 C.E., during the reign of Caligula, to the time of Gordian III (238–244 C.E.). Many of the city's coins show the infant Dionysus on Nysa's knees, Dionysus as a youth, and other gods common to city coins in general.

Nysa-Scythopolis

246a. AE 20mm. Gabinius.
    O: Bare head of Gabinius to right; inscription in field ΓAB (Gabinius).
    R: Nike holding wreath in hand advances to left, inscription is barbaric ΓABEINWN NVC (of the People of Gabinian Nysa). Meshorer 103.   750.00

247

247. AE 25mm. Nero.
    O: Laureate,   undraped   bust   right;   inscription   around, NEPWN KΛAYΔIOΣ KAIΣAP.
    R: Tyche wearing turreted crown and long gown stands left, left hand holds sceptre, right a round object; on left, NYΣA, date in field, LPA (Year 101). Struck 54–55 C.E. BMC 1, Ros. 7.   400.00

248. AE 24mm. Gordian III.
    O: Laureate bust right wearing paludamentum; inscription around,
    AVTK M ANT.ΓOPΔIANOC CEB.
    R: Tyche wearing turreted crown and long gown sits right on chair-
    like throne and nurses the infant Dionysus; inscription around,
    NVC CKVΘO IEP ACY, ΔT (of Nysa Scythopolis, holy
    city of asylum, 304). Struck 241 C.E. BMC 6 var, Ros. 55.
                                                                450.00
249. AE 26mm. Gordian III.
    O: Laureate bust right wearing paludamentum; inscription around,
    AVT K M ANT ΓOPΔIANOC CEB.
    R: Young Dionysus nude, with scarf flying behind, advancing right
    with thyrsus in right hand and left hand on head of small fig-
    ure, to left a panther looks upward; inscription around,
    NVC CKVΘ IEP ACY, date across field, Δ T, and
    grapes in field above right. BMC 12, Ros. 59.   450.00

Sebaste (Samaria, Shomron)

*And he bought the hill Samaria of Shemer for two talents of silver; and
he built on the hill, and called the name of the city which he built, after
the name of Shemer, the owner of the hill, Samaria.* (1 Kings 16:24)

Sebaste, also known as Samaria, and the biblical Shomron, was capital of
the ancient kingdom of Israel.

The city sits on a strategic hill that gives access to Meggido in the north,
the coastal plain in the west, and Jerusalem and the Jordan River in the
east.

In 332 B.C.E. it was captured by Alexander the Great, who settled
Macedonian soldiers there. In 108 B.C.E. John Hyrcanus I captured and
destroyed the city, converting its Samaritan residents to Judaism by force.
In 63 B.C.E. Pompey annexed Samaria to Syria and a few years later
Gabinius rebuilt the city extensively.

Augustus, in 30 B.C.E., gave the city to Herod I, who named it Sebaste
in honor of the emperor (Sebastos is Greek for Augustus). Herod built it
into one of the area's most magnificent cities, modeled in the Greco-Roman
tradition and topped off with a temple to Caesar Augustus. Josephus says
that this temple could be seen gleaming white in the sun from the Mediterranean sea, 20 miles away.

During the reign of Septimius Severus, Sebaste was made a Roman colony with the title "Lucia Septimia Sebaste." Eventually, the city lost most of its political power because of its geographical proximity to Neapolis.

The coinage of Sebaste begins with Nero and ends with Elagabalus. Many of the coins of Domitian struck here are found with the countermark of the Tenth Roman Legion. The reverse types of Sebaste's coins often show the city-goddess Tyche, the Temple of Augustus, and the Rape of Persephone. Sebaste's era is dated from 25 B.C.E.

Sebaste

250.   AE 24mm. Domitian.
       O: Laureate, undraped bust right; inscription around, IMPDOM-
          ITI . . . CAESAR.
       R: Bearded male stands right, his right hand holding sceptre and
          Nike in left, Nike stands left offering a crown; inscription around,
          CEBACTHNWN, field above right LΘP. Struck 84–85 C.E.
          BMC 5, Ros. 7.   300.00
251.   AE 23mm. Julia Maesa.
       O: Draped bust right wearing stephane; inscription around,
          MAESA   AVGVSTA.
       R: Rape of Persephone—Hades rides in galloping quadriga right,
          he carries Persephone in right arm, Eros flies right above; in-
          scription, COL.L.SEP, in ex., SEBASTE. BMC 16, Ros.
          30.   375.00

Neapolis (Nablus, Shechem)

> *And Abram passed through the land unto the place of Shechem, unto
> the terebinth of Moreh.* (Genesis 12:6)

Neapolis, the modern Nablus, has always been an urban center of the Samarian region. It was founded by Vespasian in 72 C.E. near the site of ancient Shechem. The local era dates from this event. In the Bible Shechem is first mentioned in connection with Abraham's arrival in Canaan. Indeed, archaeological evidence indicates that the city did exist in the Middle Bronze Age II—the time of the Patriarchs.

Neapolis lies on the "neck" between Mount Gerizim and Mount Ebal. It became the capital of the Samaritan sect after the Exile until it was destroyed in 128 B.C.E. by John Hyrcanus I. After being rebuilt the city was destroyed again following the First Revolt. After the Bar Kochba War, Hadrian replaced the Samaritan Temple on Mt. Gerizim with a temple to Zeus Hypsistos. Because of his fondness for the city, Vespasian honored it with his family name, "Flavia".

The classic coin type of Neapolis shows the two peaks of the city, with a large temple standing on one of them. Considerable detail is shown, with stairways, altars, and columns. In fact, archaeologists have used the coin scenes to locate ancient structures.

The coinage of Neapolis began under Domitian in 82–83 C.E. and ended about 254 C.E. during the reign of Volusianus. During the struggle for power between Pescennius Niger and Septimius Severus, the Samaritans of Neapolis took the side of Niger. When Severus won and became emperor, he punished Neapolis by taking away many of its political rights. Among these was the right to mint coins; thus the city issued none during the reign of Severus, 193–211 C.E.

In addition to scenes of Mt. Gerizim and its surroundings, the coin types of Neapolis show cult figures, temples, and sacrificial scenes.

Neapolis

252. AE 25mm. Domitian.
O: Laureate, undraped bust right; inscription around, ΑVΤΟΚ ΔΟΜΙΤΙΑΝΟΣ ΚΑΙΣΑΡ ΣΕΒΑΣΤΟΣ.
R: Inscription and date within a wreath, tied below, ΦΛΑΟVΙ ΝΕΑΠΟΛΙ ΣΑΜΑΡΕ ΛΑΙ. (Flavia Neapolis which is in Samaria, Year 11). Struck 81 C.E. BMC 2, Ros. 1.   400.00

252

253

257

253. AE 34mm. Antonius Pius.

O: Laureate bust right wearing paludamentum and euirass; inscription around, AVTOK KAICAP ANTWNINOC CEBA CEVCE.

R: Mt. Gerizim with arched colonnade, roadway, shrines, altar and temple; inscription around, ΦΛΝΕΑCΠΟΛΕWCVPIAC ΠΑΛΑICΤΙΝHC, ET ΠZ. (Flavia Neapolis which is in Syria Palestina, Year 88). Struck 158–159 C.E. BMC 22.   400.00

254. AE 23mm. Marcus Aurelius.

O: Bareheaded, undraped bust right; inscription around, AYPHΛ IOC KAICAP EVCEBCEBV.

R: Zeus Heliopolites, mummy-like figure flanked by foreparts of two bulls, in right hand a whip, in left two ears of corn; inscription around, ΦΛ ΝΕΑCΠΟΛΕWC CVPIAC ΠΑΛΕCΤΙΝHC, across field, date ET ΠΗ. Struck 159–160 C.E. BMC 31, Ros. 15.   325.00

255. AE 27mm. Faustina Jr.

O: Draped bust right, hair in chignon, inscription beginning below left, ΦΑYCΤΕΙΝΑ CEB EY CEBAΘYΓA.

R: Tyche wearing turreted crown and long chiton stands to front, looks left, cornucopia in left hand, right hand rests on rudder; inscription, ΦΛ ΝΕΑCΠΟΛΕ CYPIAC ΠΑΛΕCΤΙ, date across field ET ΠΗ. BMC 54, Ros. 20.   300.00

256. AE 22mm. Elagabalus.

O: Laureate bust right wearing paludamentum and cuirass; inscription around, AVTK MAVP ANTWNINOC.

R: Tetrastyle temple, Tyche stands left in central arch, she holds small bust and leans on spear; inscription around, ΦΛ ΝΕΑCΠ ΟΛΕW CVP Π. BMC 104, Ros. 44.   325.00

257. AE 25.5mm. Treb. Gallus.

O: Bust right wearing paludamentum and cuirass; inscription around, AVT.KAI.Γ.OVETPEBΓΑΛOC.

R: Mt. Gerizim with colonnade, steps, road, and shrines, supported by eagle standing with wings spread; inscription around ΦΛ ΝΕΑCΠΟΛΕWC. BMC 149, Ros. 113.   450.00

Antipatris (Aphek)

Then the soldiers, as it was commanded them, took Paul, and brought him by night to Antipatris. (Acts 23:31)

Ruins of the ancient city Aphek, later called Antipatris, lie near the modern town of Petah Tikvah at the source of the Yarkon River. It was one of the cities mentioned in a list of Canaanite cities captured by Tuthmosis III (1504–1450 B.C.E.).

In Biblical times the king of Aphek was one of the 31 rulers of Canaan vanquished by Joshua. And it was at Aphek that the Philistines gathered their armies in preparation to do battle with Israel.

The city was key in early warfare because it stood at a junction of important highways that led to Jerusalem, Caesarea, and Joppa. In 132 B.C.E. the city was conquered by John Hyrcanus I.

Antipatris was founded by Herod I and named after Antipater, his father. Under Herod the city became the center of a district surrounded by several prosperous villages.

M. Rosenberger lists only three coin types of Antipatris, two issued under Elagabalus (218–222 C.E.) and one under Julia Maesa.

Antipatris

258.   AE 17mm. Elagabalus.
O: Laureate bust right wearing paludamentum and cuirass; inscription around, AVT K LM AVP ANTWNINOC.
R: Tetrastyle temple, Tyche standing left within central arch, she wears short gown, left hand rests on spear and right holds bust; in ex. AN ANTI. Ros. 1.   500.00

Joppa (Jaffa, Yafo)

> *I was in the city of Joppa praying: and in a trance I saw a vision, A certain vessel descend, as it had been a great sheet, let down from heaven by four corners.* (Acts 11:5)

The city of Joppa, modern Jaffa, is another of Israel's most ancient, having a recorded history of more than 3,000 years.

It was supposedly off Joppa's shores that Jonah was swallowed by the whale.

Since it was the main port for Jerusalem and the rest of inland Judaea, Joppa was frequently conquered. Sennacherib, king of Assyria, took it in 701 B.C.E. on his way to fight Hezekiah, king of Judah, and his Egyptian allies; Alexander the Great occupied it in 332 B.C.E. In about 301 B.C.E. it fell into the hands of the Ptolemies and soon became a Greek city along with many others in the area.

Judah Maccabee attacked Joppa and burned the harbor in retaliation for the drowning of some 200 Jews.

When Pompey conquered the area in 66 B.C.E., Joppa became a free city under the Syrian governor. In 38 B.C.E., as Herod I traveled to Jerusalem to establish his rule, he captured Joppa. It was taken from him and given to Cleopatra during Antony's reign, but Herod regained it under Augustus.

During the First Revolt Joppa was destroyed by the forces of Cestius Gallus, but rebel Jews quickly rebuilt the town—only to have it crushed again by Vespasian, who fortified it with a Tenth Legion guard and rebuilt the city.

According to legend Perseus rescued the princess Andromeda from a cliff off Joppa's coast. For this reason Athena, the patron goddess of Perseus, appears on all of the city coins.

Many Ptolemaic coins were also minted here. Apparently, the only Imperial coins struck here were during the reign of Elagabalus (218–222 C.E.).

Joppa

259. AE 21mm. Elagabalus.
O: Laureate, draped bust right; surrounded by inscription, AVT K MA ANTNEINOC CEB.
R: Athena stands right wearing long gown, she rests right hand on spear and holds shield in left; surrounded by inscription, ΦΛΑ ΙΟΠΠΗC. (Flavia Joppe). Ros. 9, BMC 1.   800.00

Diospolis (Lydda, Lod)

> But when Cestius had marched from Antipatris to Lydda, he found the city empty of its men.   (Josephus, Wars II, XIX:1)

The inclusion of Lydda's name on a list of the towns of Canaan captured by Tuthmosis III)1504–1450 B.C.E.) testifies to its antiquity. Today it is the home of Israel's Ben Gurion airport and lies 11 miles southeast of Tel-Aviv.

During Hellenistic times the city was not within Judaea, but Demetrius I gave it to Jonathan the Hasmonean in 145 B.C.E.

During the days of the Maccabees it became purely a Jewish town. On his way to Jerusalem in 66 C.E. the Roman proconsul of Syria, Cestius Gallus, burned Lydda. It only regained its importance after Jerusalem fell. Lydda then became a haven for sages and teachers and remained an important Jewish learning center for some 300 years, especially in Talmudic times.

Under Roman rule the town grew and Septimius Severus made it a colony, renaming it "Colonia Lucia Septima Severa Diospolis" (Diospolis means "City of Zeus"). The city's local era begins in 199–200 C.E.

Coins of Diospolis were apparently minted from the time of Julia Domna (wife of Septimius Severus) through the reign of Elagabalus. The city goddess Tyche, Zeus, and Demeter are among the gods and goddesses depicted.

260

Diospolis-Lydda

260. AE 25mm. Julia Domna.
   O: Draped bust right, her hair curled; inscription around, IOVΛI. ΔOMNA.CEBAC.
   R: Draped bust Sarapis right wearing kalathos; inscription around, Λ.CEΠ.CEOV ΔIOCΠOΛIC, date on sides of head, EI. (Lucia Septimia Severa Diospolis, year 10). Struck 208–209 C.E. BMC 1, Ros. 2.   700.00

Nicopolis (Emmaus)

Be diligent to come unto me to Nicopolis.   (Titus 3:12)

In modern Israel the city once known as Emmaus, later Nicopolis, lies near Latrun on the road from Jaffa to Jerusalem, about nine miles southeast of Lydda.

During the Persian period the city was also known as Hamthan, or "Hot Springs." In 166 B.C.E., near Emmaus, Judah Maccabee won a great victory over the Seleucid army of Gorgias and Nikanor. After the battle Judah proceeded on to Jerusalem.

In 68 C.E., after the destruction of Jerusalem, Vespasian settled a number of soldiers from the Legio V. Macedonia here. In 221 C.E. Elagabalus renamed the city Nicopolis, or "the city of victory," and the local era dates from this event.

Coins were issued by Nicopolis-Emmaus from the time of Faustina I to that of Elagabalus (218–222 C.E.). Regarding the types of coins issued by this city, G. Hill notes that they "are of no special interest, being of the kind characteristic of this part of Palestine."

262

Nicopolis-Emmaus

261.   Coin omitted.

262.   AE 26mm. Elagabalus.
O: Bust right wearing paludamentum and cuirass; inscription
around, M AV ANTWNINOC.
R: Eagle supporting wreath upon spread wings; inscription within,
NEIKO.ΠΟΛΙC; inscription around, ANTWNIN. . . .
ΠΟΛΕWC, and date between eagle's legs EB (Year 2).
Struck 221–222 C.E. BMC 6.   1,000.00

Aelia Capitolina (Jerusalem)

*Pray for the peace of Jerusalem; May they prosper that love thee. Peace
be within thy walls, And prosperity within thy palaces.*   (Psalms 122:6, 7)

Aelia Capitolina was the name of Jerusalem for several hundred years,
from the end of the Bar Kochba War to the Arab conquest of the land in
the seventh century C.E.

When Titus succeeded in destroying the Temple in 70 C.E., the Jewish
community was dispersed from the city. In fact, a camp of the Tenth Roman
Legion was established upon the Temple Mount.

However, Jerusalem was again occupied by Jews in 132 C.E., upon the
beginning of the Bar Kochba Revolt against Rome. Among other things,
this revolt had been sparked by Hadrian's decision to rebuild the city as
a Roman colony to be called Aelia Capitolina. The name was derived from
the fact that Hadrian intended to (and did) build a temple to Jupiter
Capitolinus in the city. Aelius was a family name of Hadrian's (Aelius
Hadrianus).

Aelia Capitolina was probably not established until after Bar Kochba
and his men fell in the battle of Betar in 135, although it was founded
earlier, during Hadrian's visit to the Land of Israel in 130 C.E. Once the
city was re-named, Jews were forbidden even to approach it, except perhaps
on the Ninth of Ab. Hadrian had the city populated largely with legionary
veterans.

Aelia Capitolina issued its own coins from about 135 C.E. until the reign of Valerian (253–260). Aelia's coins are rich with symbolism of the Sixth and Tenth Roman Legions, including the boar, the galley, and the eagle. Other gods as well as temple facades are commonly found.

Many Jewish coins were also minted in Jerusalem, but of course they are not to be included in the "City Coin" series.

Aelia Capitolina

263. AE 24mm. Hadrian.
  O: Laureate bust right wearing paludamentum and cuirass; inscription around, IMP CAES TRAIANO HADRIANO AVG PP.
  R: Hadrian as founder ploughing right with cow and bull; inscription from above left, COL.AEL.KAPIT, in ex. COND. Kad. 1, Ros. 1.   500.00

264. AE 22mm. Antonius Pius.
  O: Laureate bust right wearing paludamentum and cuirass; inscription around, IMP ANTONINVS AVG PPP.
  R: The Dioscuri standing to front looking at each other, inner hands on hips, outer holding spears, an eagle stands between them; inscription, CO AE CA. BMC 21. Kad. 22.   275.00

265. AE 14/15mm. Antonius Pius.
  O: Laureate, bearded bust right wearing paludamentum and cuirass; inscription around, IMP CAES T A ANTONINO.
  R: Boar walking right, above, K A C. BMC 29, Kad. 33, Ros. 19.   225.00

266. AE 23mm. Antonius Pius.
  O: Laureate draped bust wearing paludamentum; inscription around, IMP ANTONINVS AVG PPP.
  R: Tetrastyle temple, Tyche standing left within central arch, a spear in left hand and a bust in right, with foot resting on a helmet, in exergue, C A C. Kad. 12, Ros. 10.   250.00

266   267

267. AE 23mm. Elagabalus.
      O: Laureate bust right wearing paludamentum and cuirass; inscription around, IMP C MA ANTONIN . . .
      R: Quadriga draws cart carrying stone of Elagabal, wavy line in ex., inscription above, COL ACCP F. BMC 85, Kad. 146.   350.00

Raphia (Rafah)

Alexander recovered this blow, and turned his forces towards the maritime parts, and took Raphia and Gaza, with Anthedon also. (Josephus, *Wars*, I, IV:2)

Raphia, how known as Rafah, is at the southeastern tip of ancient Judaea. Today it is at the southern part of the Gaza Strip.

The city is first mentioned in an inscription of the Pharoah Seti I (c. 1300 B.C.E.) as "Rph". The city is not mentioned in the Bible.

Here, in 217 B.C.E., Ptolemy IV defeated Antiochus III (the Great). Later the city was conquered by Alexander Jannaeus, but it was freed from Jannaeus's rule by Pompey and rebuilt by Gabinius. The town's era dates from 57 B.C.E.

Raphia's city coinage begins with Commodus (180 C.E.) and ends with Philip I (244–245 C.E.). Since the city was the seat of worship of Isis and Dionysus, they frequently appear on the coins. Tyche, Zeus, Artemis, Apollo, and others are also depicted. An interesting coin of Gordian III carries the image of a Sphinx. This may relate to the fact that Raphia was an ancient stopping point before embarking across the desert in caravans for Egypt.

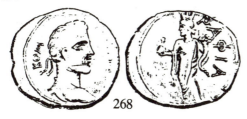

268

Raphia

268.   AE 28mm. Commodus.
O: Laureate bust right; inscription around, AYT.M.ANT. KOM.CEB.
R: Tyche wearing turreted crown stands to left and holds cornucopia in left hand and infant Dionysus seated on right; inscription PAΦIAMC (Year 240). Struck 180–181 C.E. BMC 1.   350.00

269.   AE 23/24mm. Severus Alexander.
O: Laureate bust right wearing paludamentum and cuirass; inscription around, AVTK M AVP CEOV AΛEΞANΔPOC.
R: Zeus seated left on throne with left hand resting on sceptre and holding Nike in right, Nike stands right holding wreath out to him; inscription, PAΦIA AΠC (Year 281). Struck 221–222 C.E. BMC 7.   300.00

Eleutheropolis (Beit Guvrin)

Eleutheropolis, or Beit Guvrin, lies halfway between Jerusalem and Gaza.

Septimius Severus once visited the city and gave it the privileges of a Roman city; hence it became known as Eleutheropolis, "the city of liberty."

According to the Midrash, Eleutheropolis was the Biblical "Mount Sur of the Horites." It is a conclusion apparently derived because of a play on words, since "hori" means both "free men" and "cave dweller." There are many large caves in the area of Eleutheropolis.

The local era of this city begins in 199–200 C.E.

Coinage was struck in Eleutheropolis from the reign of Septimius Severus (193–211 C.E.) to the reign of Elagabalus (218–222 C.E.). Gods frequently depicted on the coins include Zeus, Nike, Roma, and Athena.

Eleutheropolis

270.   AE 27mm. Septimius Severus.
O: Laureate, bearded bust right with paludamentum and cuirass; inscription around, AK Λ CE CEOVEV . . .
R: Tetrastyle temple with Tyche wearing turreted crown and long gown standing left within central arch, she holds bust in extended right hand, cornucopia in left, river god swims below her feet; inscription, on left ΛCEΠ, right CEO, in exergue EΛEVO, flanking Tyche EΘ. Ros. 8.   400.00

271

271. AE 25mm. Elagabalus.
O: Laureate bust right wearing paludamentum and cuirass; surrounded by inscription, AVTK ANTWNEINOC CE.
R: Tetrastyle temple with Tyche wearing turreted crown and long gown standing left within central arch, she holds bust in extended right hand, cornucopia in left, river god swims below her feet; inscription, Λ CEΠ CEOV, in ex., EΛEYΘ, date flanks Tyche, EΘI (Lucia Septimia Severa Eleutheropolis, Year 19). Struck 217–218 C.E. Ros. 25, BMC 5.   550.00

Anthedon

> *Alexander [Jannaeus] recovered this blow, and turned his forces towards the maritime parts, and took Raphia and Gaza, with Anthedon also.* (Josephus, *Wars*, I, IV:2)

About two miles northwest of Gaza, on the Mediterranean coast, lay the ancient Greek city of Anthedon. Its name means "flower city" in Greek.

It was one of the southern areas conquered by Alexander Jannaeus and later retaken by Pompey. In 55 B.C.E. the city was rebuilt by the Syrian proconsul Gabinius.

Anthedon was one of the cities that Augustus gave Herod I as a reward for his loyalty during Augustus's war with Antony and Cleopatra. Grateful for the gift, and always ready to flatter one in power, the politically astute Herod renamed the city Agrippias or Agrippeion in honor of general Marcus Vipsanius Agrippa, son-in-law of Augustus.

During the First Revolt the Zealots attacked Anthedon, but they were repulsed and the city remained Hellenized.

City coins were minted in Anthedon from the reign of Septimius Severus (191–211 C.E.) through Severus Alexander (222–236 C.E.). The reverse types of Anthedon's coins depict Tyche, the city goddess, sometimes within a temple. The local era begins in 219–220 C.E.

272

Anthedon

272. AE 24mm. Elagabalus.
O: Laureate bust right; inscription around, AVT K M AN-
TWNINOC.
R: Tyche stands left within tetrastyle temple, she wears turreted
crown and holds sceptre in left hand and bust in right, right foot
on prow; inscription, ET Γ . . . , in ex. ANΘHΔO. Ros. 1
var.   500.00

Gaza

*And Samson went to Gaza, and saw there a harlot, and went in unto
her.*   (Judges 16:1)

Gaza lies south of Ascalon on the coast of the Mediterranean. It was a
final caravan stop before entering the desert.

Like Ascalon, Gaza was one of the Philistines' five coastal cities from
the twelfth century B.C.E.

In 332 B.C.E., after a five-month siege, Alexander the Great conquered
Gaza. Later it became the Mediterranean port of the Nabataeans, whose
caravans arrived there from Petra or Eilat.

Alexander Jannaeus attacked and besieged Gaza in 96 B.C.E., and it
surrendered after a year. Jannaeus slaughtered the majority of the population and wrecked the city. It was refounded and rebuilt under Pompey
the Great by his Syrian proconsul, Gabinius.

Augustus made a gift of the city to Herod I, and it became a separate
segment in his kingdom, under control of the governor of Idumaea.

The city continued to prosper during the Roman period. Both the Ptolemies and the Seleucids minted coins in Gaza, in addition to the traditional
city coinage.

The first city coins of Gaza were struck in 61–60 B.C.E., the beginning
of the local era. Coinage continued through the reign of Gordian III (238–
244 B.C.E.). The mintmark of the city of Gaza is ꓭ or "mem" from the
Phoenician alphabet. This is the first initial of the name Marnas, as Zeus
was called by the people of Gaza. He was a special local god. Other coins
of Gaza show the god Minos, the goddesses Tyche and Io, temples, and,
on the early coinage, the cornucopia. Coins were also minted in Gaza
during the Persian, Ptolemaic, and Seleucid periods.

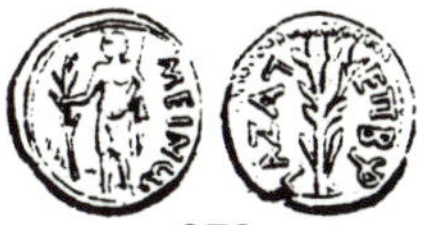

273

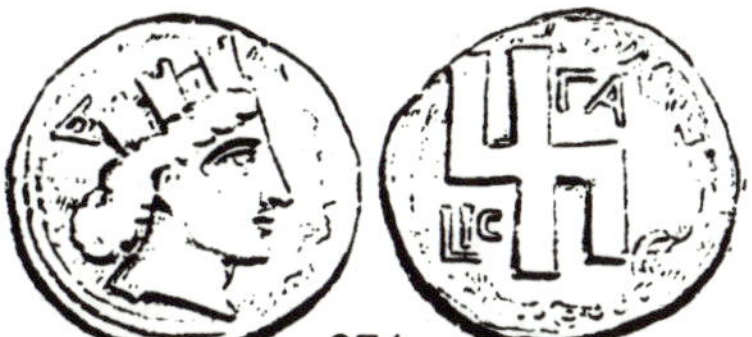

274

Gaza

272a. AR fraction Philisto-Arabian (4–10mm) c. fifth century B.C.E.
O: Helmeted head to right.
R: Owl facing front, olive spray to left, to right ΑΘΕ, sometimes the mintmarks Ο or 𐤌 appear. Ros. 9–11. 150.00

273. AE 13mm.
O: Minos stands left holding spear in left hand and branch in right; inscription on right ΜΕΙΝWC.
R: Tree surrounded by inscription ΓΑΖΑΓΕΒϤΡ; in right field, 𐤌. (Year 192). Struck 131–132 C.E. BMC 8. 125.00

274. AE 23mm.
O: Tyche bust right wearing turreted crown.
R: Large 𐤌 with inscription ΓΑ in upper right, and IC in lower left. Struck 149–150 C.E. BMC 9. 150.00

275. AE 22mm. Augustus.
O: Bareheaded, undraped bust right; inscription, ΚΑΙ.
R: Turreted Tyche stands left wearing long gown, holding branch in right hand, two ears of corn in left, in field left, 𐤌 , in field right, LΞC ΓΑ. Struck 6 C.E. BMC 10, Ros. 44. 125.00

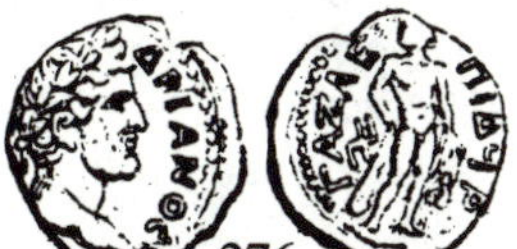

276

276. AE 16–17mm. Hadrian.
O: Laureate, draped bust right; inscription around, ΑΚΑΤΡ ΑΔΡΙΑΝΟC.
R: Heracles nude to front, looking left, right hand on club, left holds lion skin, 𐤌 in left field; inscription around, ΓΑΖΑ ΕΠΙΔϘ. Struck 133–134 B.C.E. BMC 52, Ros. 55. 150.00

277. AE 23mm. Geta.
O: Bareheaded bust right wearing paludamentum and cuirass; inscription around, Λ CΕΠ ΓΕΤΑC Κ.
R: Io is on left, facing right, and Tyche wearing turreted crown and carrying cornucopia is on right facing left. The two join hands; between them 𐤌 ; inscription around, ΕΙW ΓΑΖΑ, in ex. ΞC (Io, Gaza, year 260). Struck 199–200 C.E. BMC 136. 250.00

Ascalon (Ashkelon)

Tell it not in Gath, Publish it not in the streets of Ashkelon; Lest the daughters of the Philistines rejoice. (2 Samuel 1:20)

Ascalon is one of the oldest, largest, and most important of the ancient cities in the Land of Israel. It was a major port in ancient times, located north of Gaza on the Mediterranean Sea.

Ascalon was a Canaanite city-state under Egyptian influence during the 18th to 20th dynasties (C 1600 B.C.E.).

It later became one of the famous five coastal cities of the Philistines. Early in Hellenistic times, under the Ptolemies, Ascalon became a free port and autonomous city. Late in the second century B.C.E. the independent city of Ascalon issued silver coins.

Although they made many attempts to capture Ascalon, the Hasmoneans never succeeded. The city never belonged to Herod I either, although he built many temples, palaces, and other public buildings here.

Ascalon flourished throughout the Roman period, as today's magnificent ruins will testify, and the city was mainly Hellenistic in culture; although there was still a large Jewish community.

Coins were minted in Ascalon from about 200 B.C.E. and continued through the reign of Maximinus I (235–238 C.E.). The main types of Ascalon's coins carry designs of the city goddess Tyche, the war god Phanebal, and the galley. Temples and other gods and goddesses, including a local goddess Derketo, who was part woman and part fish, also appear on Ascalon's coins. The city's mint mark was the dove. The letters AΣ, or other abbreviations for the name of the city, also appear frequently. Ptolemaic and Seleucid coins were also minted at Ascalon. The city's coins are dated from two local eras beginning in 104 B.C.E. and 58 B.C.E.

 Ascalon
279

278.   AE 15mm. Antiochus IV (Epiphanes) 175–164 B.C.E.
       O: Bust to right, bevelled edge.
       R: Dove standing left; above, BA, below, AC . . Ros. 26.
                                                                    75.00

279.   AE 14mm.
       O: Bust Tyche right wearing turreted crown; inscription in front, ACKAΛ.
       R: War galley to right; inscription above, AKC (Year 221). Struck 117–118 C.E. Ros. 68.   50.00

280

280. AE 19mm. Domitian.
   O: Laureate, undraped bust right; in front, inscription, CEBAC.
   R: Phanebal, the war deity, stands left holding palm branch and
      shield in left hand and raised harpoon in right; inscription on
      right AC, date on left H P (Year 198). Struck 94–95 C.E.
      BMC 134.   100.00

281. AE 24/25mm. Trajan.
   O: Laureate, undraped bust right; inscription, CEBAC TOC.
   R: Tyche wearing turreted crown stands left on prow, right hand
      holds standard and left aphlaston, altar and inscription on left,
      ACKAΛΩ, on right is dove standing left and date below, IC
      (Year 210). Struck 106–107 C.E. BMC 138.   125.00

282

282. AE 27mm. Antoninus Pius.
   O: Laureate undraped bust right; inscription ANTWNINOC CE-
      BACTOC.
   R: Dekerto wearing long gown and crescent on top of head; stands
      left on a Triton which holds cornucopia aloft in hands; Dekerto
      holds dove in right hand and rests left on sceptre; inscription
      and upward on left, ACKAΛWN, date on right ENC (151–
      152 C.E.). BMC 194, Ros. 177.   225.00

283. AE 15mm. Antoninus Pius.
   O: Laureate bust right undraped; inscription ANTWNIN . . .
   R: Phanebal on base, stands facing with head right and branch,
      shield and harpoon, upward on left ACKAΛW, on right down-
      ward ΞC (156–157 C.E.). Ros. 181.   150.00

Philippopolis

Philippopolis, in northern Transjordan, was possibly the birthplace of Philip I (the Arabian) and was founded by him as a Roman colony. The first coins of this city show the deified bust of Marinos, Philip's father, who may have been worshipped here. Even though Philippopolis is a Roman colony, the coin's inscriptions are in Greek—with the exception of the two letters SC (Senatus Consulto), which are common on Roman bronze coins and indicate the Senate's approval. Only coins from Philip and his family were struck here.

Philippopolis

284. AE 30mm. Otacilia Severa.
O: Draped bust on crescent facing right, wearing stephane, her hair is waved and taken up in a long plait at back of head; inscription MAP ΩΤΑΚΙΛΙ CEOYHPAN CEB.
R: Helmeted Roma seated to left and wearing mantle and chiton, in her extended right hand is an eagle supporting two small figures, left hand rests on spear, oval shield leans on chair. SC (Senatus Consulto). Inscription, ΦΙΛΙΠΠΟΠΟΛΙΤΩΝ ΚΟΛΩΝΙΑC (of the people of Philippopolis, colonia). Rosenberger 3, Spijkerman 5.   250.00

Hippos (Susita, Tob)

> *Then Jephthah fled from his brethren, and dwelt in the land of Tob.* (Judges 11:3)

This city was known as Susita from Talmudic sources. During the Hellenistic and Roman periods the name was changed to Hippos, which is simply a Greek translation of the Hebrew word (*Sus*) for horse. Supposedly, it was so named because the hill on which it stood was shaped like a horse. (One would be hard put to see the resemblance today.)   Hippos is listed by Pliny as one of the Decapolis cities. It was also one of the towns captured and destroyed by Alexander Jannaeus, later captured and rebuilt by Pompey. Augustus added Hippos to Herod the Great's kingdom. After the Jews were massacred in 66 C.E. in Caesarea, the Jews of Hippos took revenge on the gentile inhabitants of their city. The gentiles eventually sided successfully with the Romans in the First Revolt.

Hippos

285. AE 24mm. Antinonus Pius
O: Laureate and draped bust to right; inscription, AYTOKP KYP ANTWNINOC.
R: Tyche wearing turreted crown and long chiton stands left and holds horse by bridle with right hand and cornucopia in left hand; inscription, ANTIO.TW.ΠP IΠ.THC IEP.K.ACYΛOY (of the Antiocheans at Hippos, holy city of asylum). Rosenberger 8, Spijkerman 7.   450.00

Canatha

This is the last city in Pliny's list of the Decapolis. Originally the city was named after Gabinius, who founded it, and its era begins in 63 B.C.E. according to the Pompeian era.

In Canatha, Herod the Great was defeated by the Nabataeans, who may have been the inhabitants. The modern ruins of Kh. Kanawat, near Bostra, are no doubt the ruins of the ancient Canatha.

Canatha

286. AE 18mm. Claudius.
 O: Laureate and draped bust to left.
 R: Turreted bust of Tyche to left; inscription KANAΘHNΩN BIP (of the people of Canatha 112). Struck 49 C.E. Rosenberger 2, Spijkerman 3.   175.00

287. AE 24mm. Commodus.
 O: Laureate bust of Commodus to right; inscription AVTK MA ANTO KOM.
 R: Draped Dionysos standing to left, holding thrysos with left hand and pouring wine from kantharos to panther at his feet on left; inscription ΓABEIN KANAΘ, ΓNC (Gabinian Canatha, 253). Struck 190 C.E. Rosenberger 5, Spijkerman 7.   375.00

Abila (Abel)

It happened with a water-channel in Abel that they used to draw from it on the Sabbath by the consent of the elders.   (Mishnah, Erubin, 8:7)

Even though Abila is not mentioned by Pliny among the cities of the Decapolis, it is attributed to this group. The reason is an inscription found in Tayibeh which suggests the connection. It was one of the cities conquered by Alexander Jannaeus and later by Pompey; thus it is dated from the Pompeian era beginning in 63 C.E.

The name Seleucia is also affiliated with the city because it was conquered by Antiochus III in 198 B.C.E.

During the reign of Nero, Abila was among the territories given to Agrippa II.

Early coins of Abila show a bunch of grapes, which were among its main exports.

Abila

288. AE 25mm. Lucius Verus.   288
 O: Laureate and cuirassed bust right; inscription AYT KAICAP AYP Λ OYHPOC
 R: Nude Herakles seated left on a rock, he holds a club in his left hand and rests right on rock; inscription, CE ABIΛHNWN I A A Γ KOI CV, SKC (of the people of Seleucia Abila, 282). Struck 219 C.E.   350.00

Gadara (Gader, Hammat Gader)

Then the whole multitude of the country of the Gadarenes round about besought him to depart from them.   (Luke 8:37)

The remains of the ancient town of Gadara stand today at a site called Umm Qeis, on a mountain east of the Jordan, which commands a splendid view of the Sea of Galilee, the Jordan Valley, and snow-capped Mt. Hermon. It is associated with the Biblical Gilead, also being mentioned as a Hellenistic settlement when Israel was conquered by Antiochus III.

Gadara was conquered by Alexander Jannaeus early in the first century B.C.E., but the city was soon destroyed during the war between Aristobulus II and Hyrcanus II. Pompey took the city and rebuilt it in 63 B.C.E., and many coins show that the city was named after him as "Pompeian Gadara."

Gadara was one of the Decapolis cities and had a large Jewish community throughout its existence.

After Herod the Great, Gadara was an autonomous city with the right to mint its own coins. Beginning with Augustus, Roman Imperial coins were struck here up until 240 C.E.

The first coins of Gadara bore a prow with the Greek inscription "Year one of Rome," with the bust of Herakles on the obverse. Another imporant coin of Gadara depicts a galley with an inscription referring to a "Naumachia," a festive event in which a mock naval battle symbolizing Pompey's conquest of the country was staged.

Other coins of Gadara depict temples of Zeus and Tyche and a river god of the nearby Yarmuk River. A cult of the Three Graces was apparently practiced in Gadara, and they appear on some of the city's later coins.

Gadara

289. AE 22mm. Nero.
　　　O: Laureate bust of Nero to right; inscription around, NEPΩN KAICAP.
　　　R: Tyche wearing turreted crown and long chiton stands left, in her right hand she holds a wreath, in her left a cornucopia, palm branch before her; inscription, ΓΑΔΑΡΑ L ΑΛΡ (Gadara, year 131). Struck 67–8 C.E. Rosenberger 28.　　　275.00

290

290. AE 25mm. Gordian III.
      O: Radiate and cuirassed bust to right; inscription around,   AV-
      TOKP MP ANTW ΓOPΔIANOC P.
      R: War galley with aphlaston and oars to right, oarsmen sit within;
      inscription above and below, ΠOMΠ ΓAΔAPEWN ΓT (of
      Pompeian Gadara, year 303). Struck 239–40 c.e. Rosenberger
      89.   300.00

Capitolias (Beth Reisha)

Little is known about this Decapolis city during the Roman period. The
Greek name is derived from the Hebrew *Beth Reisha* (*reisha* means head).
The Arabic name of the place is Beit er-Ras.
   Some of the coins show a Zeus figure seated inside a temple, and on
some of the coins the temple is protected by two towers.
   The local era of Capitolias begins in 98 c.e., the first year of Trajan's
rule, and continues to 219 c.e., during the rule of Elagabalus.

291

Capitolias

291. AE 26mm. Lucius Verus.
      O: Laureate and bearded bust to right; inscription around,
      AVT KAICAP Λ AYP OYHPOC.
      R: Tyche wearing turreted crown and short chiton holds bust and
      sceptre standing to left within a hexastyle temple; inscription
      KAΠITWΛIEWN I A A HΞ (of the people of Capito-
      lias, holy, city of asylum, autonomous 68). Struck 164 c.e. Ro-
      senberger 7.   600.00

Adraa (Edrei)

The Biblical Edrei, Adraa stood on the banks of the Yarmuk River. Adraa's era began in 106 C.E., when the city was made a part of the Province of Arabia.

Some coins of Adraa show the sacred stone of the Dusares, an Arab-Nabataen god related to Dionysos. Another important deity on Adraa's coins was the Yarmuk River God.

Adraa began issuing coins under Antoninus Pius and continued until 257 C.E. under Gallienus.

Adraa

292. AE 27.4mm. Marcus Aurelius.
O: Laureate bust to right; inscription around,   AVT.M.AV. ANTONINOC.
R: Stone of Dusares upon altar supported by two columns; inscription around ΔΟVCAPHC. ΘEOC. AΔPAHNWN EO (god Dusares of the people of Adraa, year 70). Struck 175 C.E. Rosenberger 1, Spijkerman 3.   350.00

Bostra (Basra)

The site of ancient Bostra is still called Basra. It was among the most important and strongest towns of the Provincia Arabia. Indeed, when Trajan founded the Provincia Arabia in 106 C.E., Bostra became the capital.

Apparently the Third Roman Legion was quartered in Bostra, and it is mentioned on some of the coins. Under Alexander Severus, Bostra was promoted to the rank of a Roman colony.

Bostra

293. AE 22mm. Hadrian.
O: Laureate bust to right; inscription,   AVTOKPATWP KAI-CAP TPAIANOC AΔPIANOC CEBACTOC.
R: Bust of Arabia to front with head right, wearing turreted crown and billowing mantle, figure of a small seated child is held in each arm; inscription,   APABIA. Rosenberger 1 (Arabia), Spijkerman 1.   125.00

293   294

294. AE 21mm. Severus Alexander.
     O: Laureate and cuirassed bust to right; inscription   IMP   CAES
        MAVR   SEV   ALEXANDER   AVG.
     R: Tyche bust wearing turreted crown to left, she is draped and a
        cornucopia behind her shoulder; inscription,   COLONIA
        BOSTRA.   Rosenberger 42, Spijkerman 50.   125.00

Dium (Dios)

> But Alexander (*Jannaeus*) *marched again to the city Dios, and took
> it.* (Josephus, *Antiquities*, 15:3)

Dium was one of the cities that was conquered by Alexander Jannaeus
and later captured and re-founded by Pompey, who incorporated it into
the Decapolis. The location of this ancient city is still unknown to scholars.
Coins were minted here only from 205 C.E., under Septimius Severus, until
220 C.E., under Elagabalus. Some of the coins depict a hexastyle temple
with an altar associated with Zeus, whose name was Dios in Greek.

295

Dium

295. AE 23mm. Geta.
     O: Bareheaded and cuirassed bust to right; inscription around,
        ΠΟΥΠC   ΓΕΤΑC.Κ
     R: War gods stands to front between two reclining bulls, holding
        eagle on standard in right hand and Nike with wreath in left;
        inscription   ΔΕΙΗΝWΝ   ΗΞC   (of the people of Dium, 268).
        Struck 205 C.E. Rosenberger 5, Spijkerman 6.   350.00

Pella (Pehal)

But Alexander [Jannaeus], when he had taken Pella, marched to Gerasa
again out of the covetous desire he had of Theodorus's possessions.
(Josephus, *Wars,* I, IV:8)

An ancient city eight miles east of Beth-Shean, Pella was first mentioned
as *Pi-hi-lim* in Egyptian texts dating to the late nineteenth century B.C.E.
It was also listed as one of the Canaanite cities of Tuthmosis III, and
elsewhere in Egyptian texts as a center for the manufacture of chariots.

During the Hellenistic period the city of Pehal was renamed Pella after
the Macedonian capital. Inscriptions on some of Pella's coins indicate that
the city may have been founded by Philip of Macedonia, father of Alexander the Great.

Pella was captured by Alexander Jannaeus, who destroyed it. Pompey
restored it and included it in the Decapolis.

When Titus destroyed Jerusalem, a Jewish-Christian community moved
to Pella. Josephus mentions clashes that occurred at Pella during that war.
Indeed, one coin of Pella, issued under Domitian, closely resembles some
coins of Agrippa II and the Judaea Capta coins, depicting Nike writing on
a shield.

The Jerusalem Talmud mentions the hot springs of Pella (Hammathade
Pehal) and the city's public baths (Nymphaeum), which appear on some
of Pella's coins.

Pella

296. AE 19mm. Domitian.
  O: Laureate bust to right; inscription around, ΑΥΤΟΚΡΑΤΩΡ
  ΔΟΜΙΤΙΑΝΟΣ ΚΑΙΣΑΡ.
  R: Nike, nude to waist, stands to right, left foot on a helmet supporting a shield on knee, and writing on it with right hand;
  inscription, L EMP ΠΕΛΛΗΝΩΝ (year 145 of the people
  of Pella). Struck 82 C.E. Rosenberger 1, Spijkerman 3. 275.00

Gerasa (Gerash)

But Alexander [Jannaeus], when he had taken Pella, marched to Gerasa again out of the covetous desire he had of Theodorus's possessions.
(Josephus, *Wars,* I, IV:8)

The first mention of this city was during the Hellenistic period when it was called "Antioch on the River Chrysorrhoas." It had probably been founded by Antiochus IV and named after him. Some of the coins, however, refer to a local tradition that the city was founded by Alexander the Great.

Gerasa was one of the cities captured by Alexander Jannaeus, and it remained a Jewish possession until the time of Pompey. Gerasa was brought into the Province of Arabia after Trajan conquered the Nabataean Kingdom in 106 C.E. Hadrian visited Gerasa in 129–30, during his visit to the East.

A Jewish community lived in Gerasa from Hasmonean times, and the ruins of a large synagogue from the Byzantine period were discovered there.

Today one can also view the remains of the great Temple of Artemis, who was the city's main goddess. Her figure, depicted as the goddess of the hunt, complete with bow and arrow, is shown on many of Gerasa's coins. Other coins of Gerasa relate to the fertility cult associated with the Chrysorrhoas River, the city's water supply.

During the time of Caracalla, the title Roman Colony was given to Gerasa, but the city's coins never reflect this honor and all the inscriptions are in Greek.

Gerasa

297. AE 25mm. Hadrian.
   O: Laureate and cuirassed bust to right; inscription around, ΔIAYT.K.TPA AΔPIANOC.CE.
   R: Draped bust of Artemis-Tyche to right, hair knotted with taenia behind head, bow in front and quiver behind shoulder, large crescent below; inscription around, APTEMIC TYXH ΓE-PACWN (Artemis Tyche of the people of Gerasa). Rosenberger 7, Spijkerman, 4.   225.00

Philadelphia (Rabbath Ammon, Amman)

Is it not in Rabbah of the children of Ammon? (Deuteronomy 3:11)

This is one of the cities listed among the Decapolis by Pliny. It was the ancient Rabbath Ammon, capital of Biblical Ammon, and its name was changed to Philadelphia by Ptolemy II Philadelphus (285–247 B.C.E.). Since the city is dated according to the Pompeian era of 63 B.C.E., he must have been involved in its history.

According to Josephus, Philadelphia was stormed by Jews at the beginning of the Jewish War Against Rome.

The ancient name of Rabbath Ammon never fully disappeared from the city and the modern Amman, capital of Jordan, was built on this site.

Philadelphia

298.   AE 25mm. Domitian.
O: Laureate bust right; inscription,   KAICAP   ΔOMITIANOC.
R: Turreted Tyche, wearing veil and earrings, to right, palm branch behind head; inscription,   L   ΓMP   ΦIΛAΔEΛΦEWN   (year 143 of the people of Philadelphia). Struck 81 C.E. Rosenberger 8, Spijkerman 10.   200.00

Esbus (Heshbon)

And Israel took all these cities; and Israel dwelt in all the cities of the Amorites, in Heshbon, and in all the towns thereof. (Numbers 21:25)

Tel Heshban is the name of the town that was called Esbus during the Roman period. The Biblical name was Heshbon. Josephus reports that Herod strengthened the city to defend the area of Peraea in eastern Transjordan.

The only coins of Esbus were struck under Elagabalus.

Esbus

299. AE 23mm. Elagabalus.
O: Laureate and cuirassed bust to right; inscription around,   AVT
K M AVP ANTONINOC.
R: Tyche wearing turreted crown and short chiton, and holding
sceptre and sacred stone, stands left within a tetrastyle temple
with a central arch; inscription   AVP   ECBOVC   (Aurelia
Esbus). Rosenberger 3, Spijkerman 3.   275.00

Medaba

*And those twelve cities which his father Alexander [Jannaeus] had taken
from the Arabians, which were these, Medaba . . .   (Josephus, Antiquities, XIV, 1:4)*

This is another city of Transjordan about which little is known. The city
is famous because of the mosaic map of the Holy Land discovered here
on the floor of a Byzantine building.

A Jewish community lived here during the period of the Mishnah.

Coins were issued in Medaba from 210 to 222 C.E.

Medaba

300. AE 30. Septimius Severus.
O: Laureate and cuirassed bust to right; inscription   AVT   KAIC
CEOVHPOC.
R: Radiate helios holding reins and torch, right hand raised, in
quadriga charging to front; inscription,   AΓ   I   HΛ   I
MHΔAB   PE   (holy Helios, Medaba, 105). Struck 210 C.E.
Rosenberger 2, Spijkerman 2.   550.00

Rabbath-Moba (Rabbath-Moab)

What of Ammon and Moab in the Seventh Year?   (*Yadaim* 4:3)

According to Josephus, this city, then called Arabata, was among those of eastern Transjordan that were conquered by Alexander Jannaeus. It may also be the same as the Biblical Ir-Moab.

In the Roman-Byzantine period the city was also called Areopolis or Arsapolis; its ruins today are called Rabbah, 18 kilometers north of Kerak in Jordan.

The names Areopolis or Arsapolis mean "the city of Ariel" or "the city of Ares." This was connected with Ares, the Greek war god, who appears on many of the coins.

Rabbath-Moba

301.   AE 27mm. Septimius Severus.
     O: Laureate and cuirassed bust to right; inscription   AVT   KAC
       CEOVHPOC.
     R: Ares wearing helmet, cuirass and boots, holding upright sword
       in left hand and spear and shield in right, he stands facing on
       square stand, which is flanked by horned altars; inscription,
       PABAΘ   MWBA. Spijkerman 6.   475.00

Carach-Moba (Kir Haroshet, Kir Moab)

For the sweet cakes of Kir-hareseth shall ye mourn.   (Isaiah 16:7)

The ancient Kir Moab was the capital of the kingdom of Moab. In the Bible the city is also referred to as Kir-Haroshet. Today the place is called el-Kerak, and it is 129 kilometers south of Amman.

Many references to this city were found on a group of clay-seal impressions from a tomb at Kurnub (Mampsis), where it is called "Charachmoabapolis".

Coins were issued here only during the reign of Elagabalus.

Charach-Moba

302. AE 20mm. Elagabalus.
     O: Laureate bust right; inscription A K M AV ANTWNI-
     NOC.
     R: On right is figure seated left, before altar, which has steps leading
     up to it, on altar are the sacred stones of Dusares; inscription,
     XAP   (Char). Rosenberger 2, Spijkerman 5.   450.00

Petra

> *And brought him to the city called Petra, where the palace of Aretas
> was.*   (Josephus, *Antiquities*, XIV, 1:4)

Petra remained the capital of the Nabataeans until 106 C.E. when it was
annexed to the Roman Empire as part of the newly created Provincia
Arabia. The city was founded in the second century B.C.E.

Its mint mark on coins was a small circle, which represented the meaning
of the town's Hebrew name, *Reqem*—a round spot.

Some coins were minted here begining with the creation of the Provincia
Arabia, similar to the earlier Nabataean issues. Regular coinage began
only after the city was visited by Hadrian and it became a Metropolis.
Under Elagabalus, Petra was promoted to the full status of a Roman
colony.

Petra

303. AE 26mm. Hadrian.
     O: Laureate and cuirassed bust to right, gorgoneion on breast; in-
     scription, AVTOKPATWP KAICAP TPAIANOC AΔ-
     PIANOC CEBACTOC.
     R: Tyche wearing turreted crown, veil, mantle, and long chiton,
     sits left on rock, her right hand is extended and her left holds a
     trophy; inscription, ΠETPA MHTPOΠOΛIC (Petra
     Metropolis).   200.00

11. COINS OF NEW TESTAMENT TIMES

There are scores of references to coins and money in the New Testament. This makes for interesting study and speculation, but rarely do we know specifically which coin is referred to. In this type of work, one must guard against a literalist approach, since, as Father de Vaux, the Dominican priest, has noted: "Archaeology [or in this case, numismatics] does not confirm the text, which is what it is; it can only confirm the interpretation that we give it."

Biblical references to coins can rarely pinpoint a single coin. Rather, we read the text and attempt to extrapolate based upon other available information, including the work of other scholars.

Our goal here is to examine some of the references to money in the New Testament and to identify the coins involved as accurately as possible.

The Tribute Penny

> Is it lawful to give tribute to Caesar, or not? Shall we give, or shall we not give? But He, knowing their hypocrisy, said unto them, Why tempt ye me? Bring me a penny, that I may see it. And they brought it. And He saith unto them, Whose is this image and superscription? And they said unto Him, Caesar's. And Jesus, answering, said unto them, Render to Caesar the things that are Caesar's and to God the things that are God's. (Mark 12:14–17)

The story of the Tribute Penny may be the best-known Biblical reference to a coin. Since Tiberius reigned during the ministry of Jesus, it is logical to assume that Mark's reference is to a "penny" of Tiberius.

Except for two reverse types used on coins by Tiberius for the first two years of his reign, he employed only one type until his death in 37 C.E. This type of coin carries a portrait of the emperor on the obverse, along with the inscription TI CAESAR DIVI AVG F AVGVSTVS (Tiberius, Caesar Augustus, Son of the Divine Augustus)—hence his "image and superscription." The reverse of these coins show a seated female figure, with the inscription PONTIF MAXIM, or High Priest, another of the emperor's titles and later a title of the Bishop of Rome. Thus this type of coin is commonly referred to as the Tribute Penny: in the 1611 King James translation of the Bible, it was mistakenly translated as a penny, and so it has been called ever since. This came about because in Anglo-Saxon England, the Latin word *denarius* was transformed into the word "Penny"—the standard silver denomination (Denarius = denomination = penny). The translators simply assumed that their current money was the same money used and referred to in the Bible. For hundreds of years the British have used the initial "d" (referring to denarius) as an abbreviation for penny or pence.

The Greek equivalent to the silver denarius was the drachm, which was the same size and value. Drachms, as well as denarii, are commonly found in archaeological excavations in the Holy Land. Here are some of the interesting references to this denomination:

Luke 15:8–9. This is the parable of the woman sweeping her house for the lost piece of silver. The coin was probably a denarius or a drachm. Rogers notes that if the coin was contemporary, it was probably a Roman denarius or a drachm of Caesarea in Cappadocia, which was a major Imperial mint of the East.

Matthew 18:28. "But the same servant went out, and found one of his fellow servants, which owed him a hundred pence: and he laid hands on him, and took him by the throat, saying, Pay me that thou owest."

Matthew 20: 2, 9, 10, 13. This is the parable of the laborers in the vineyard: "And when he had agreed with the laborers for a penny a day, he sent them into his vineyard."

Mark 6:37. "He answered and said unto them, Give ye them to eat. And they say unto him, Shall we go and buy two hundred pennyworth of bread, and give them to eat?" (See also John 6:7.)

Mark 14:4–5. Judas asks about the value of the alabaster box of spikenard which the woman broke over Jesus's feet at Bethany: "Why was this waste of the ointment made? For it might have been sold for more than three hundred pence . . ." (See also John 12:5.)

Luke 7:41. Jesus puts the parable question to Simon: "There was a certain creditor which had two debtors: the one owed five hundred pence, and the other fifty. And when they had nothing to pay, he frankly forgave them both. Tell me therefore, which of them will love him most?"

Luke 10:35. In the parable of the good Samaritan: "He took out two pence, and gave them to the host, and said unto him, Take care of him; and whatsoever thou spendest more, when I come again, I will repay thee."

Revelation 6:6. "A measure of wheat for a penny, and three measures of barley for a penny; and see thou hurt not the oil and the wine."

The Tribute Penny

304

304.   AR denarius.
O: Laureate bust of Tiberius to right; inscription, TI CAESAR DIVI AVG F AVGVSTVS.
R: Female figure sits on a plain chair to right, she holds olive branch in her left hand and long sceptre in her right; inscription, PONTIF MAXIM.   300.00
Cohen 16.

The Poor Widow's Mites

> *And Jesus sat over against the treasury, and beheld how the people cast money into the treasury: and many that were rich cast in much. And there came a certain poor widow, and she threw in two mites, which make a farthing. And he called unto him his disciples, and saith unto them, Verily I say unto you, That this poor widow hath cast more in, than all they which have cast into the treasury: For all they did cast in of their abundance; but she of her want did cast in all that she had . . ."* (Mark 12:41–44)

Since Jesus made a point of how poor this widow was, and what a pittance she threw into the treasury, there is little doubt that the "Widow's mites" were the smallest coins in circulation in Jerusalem at the time. Even though the tiny bronze coins of Alexander Jannaeus (nos. 12, 13) were minted long before this episode, archaeological evidence tells us that they circulated well after Jesus died.

There is another reference to the "mite" in Luke 12:59:

> *Thou shalt not depart thence, till thou hast paid the very last mite.*

Farthing

The farthing is another denomination mentioned in the King James version; of course, it was a common English denomination in the seventeenth century. The Greek word translated as farthing was *assarion*. We suspect that this was a quadrans, even though some have suggested it to be the equivalent of the Roman "as." The bronze coins struck at Antioch were abundant, and commonly circulated in the Holy Land.

> Matthew 5:26. "Till thou has paid the uttermost farthing."
>
> Matthew 10:29. "Are not two sparrows sold for a farthing?"
>
> Luke 12:6. "Are not five sparrows sold for two farthings?"

The 30 Pieces of Silver

> *Then one of the 12, called Judas Iscariot, went unto the chief priests, and said unto them, What will ye give me, and I will deliver him unto you? And they covenanted with him for 30 pieces of silver.* (Matthew 26:14–15)

Since the silver shekels minted in the Phoenecian coastal city of Tyre were the only currency acceptable at the Jerusalem Temple, they attained a semi-official status.

Shekels of Tyre

Struck in Tyre

305. AR, 14gm. (Approximate weight). Shekel.
O: Laureate head of Melqarth to right, wearing lion skin knotted around his neck.
R: Eagle standing left with right foot on prow of ship, palm branch over right shoulder, date and club are in field to left, a Phoenician letter between eagle's legs, in right field are letters or monogram; inscription, ΤΥΡΟΥΙΕΡΑΣ ΚΑΙΑΣΥΛΟΥ (of Tyre the holy and inviolable). The dates range from A (126–5 B.C.E.) to PZ (19–18 B.C.E.).   275.00
306. AR, 7 gm. (Approximate weight). Half shekel.
O: Just as no. 305 above.
R: Just as no. 305 above.   275.00

Struck in Jerusalem

> *Silver, whenever mentioned in the Pentateuch, is Tyrian silver. What is a Tyrian silver [coin]? It is a Jerusalemite. (Tosephta Kethuboth 13:20).*

307. AR, 14gm. (Approximate weight). Shekel.
O: Just as no. 305 above, but of a generally cruder fabric and style.
R: Just as no. 305 above, but of a generally cruder style, plus the Greek letters KP to the right of the eagle. The dates range from PH (18–17 B.C.E.) to P E (69–70 C.E.).   225.00
308. AR, 7gm, (Approximate weight). Half shekel.
O: Just as no. 307 above.
R: Just as no. 307 above.   225.00

Other New Testament References to Money

The Reverend Edgar Rogers noted that Jesus often drew "a lesson from the common use and existence of money. For Him it is part of human life and human intercourse and therefore it is the concern of God. For the Numismatist his study accordingly acquires an importance and a sanction, which dignify it as nothing else can."

According to Rogers's study, here are two more notes on references to money in the New Testament.

Matthew 28:12, 15. Here reference is made to money used to bribe the soldiers who had fled from their watch at the Holy Sepulchre on Easter morning to keep silence. The reference is to large silver coins, probably the same staters or tetradrachms as the 30 pieces of silver.

Matthew 17:24. This is the story of the coin in the fish's mouth. Rogers concludes it was a tetradrachm. We observe that it would have had to have been a mighty big fish to accommodate such a large coin. Based on the fishes we have seen coming out of the Sea of Galilee, we would consider a denarius or a drachm, the Greek equivalent of a denarius, as more of a possibility.

Indeed, recent theories point to the probability that after 19 B.C.E. these shekels ceased to be minted at Tyre and were, in fact, minted in Jerusalem for use by the Jews in the Temple—a use they had already made of them for many years. Meshorer observes that the majority of the Tyre shekels after this date "were found in Israel . . . . [they] were apparently struck under Herod and his successors . . . The style and provenance of these coins as well as the literary sources which mention them, all indicate that Jerusalem was their place of origin."

This evidence makes it logical to assume that the 30 pieces of silver paid to Judas were of this currency. However, it is certainly possible that other silver coins were involved in the transaction. Other coins that commonly circulated in Israel at the time were silver tetradrachms of Antioch, as well as those of the Ptolemaic and Seleucid Kings.

Historian Michael Grant concludes that payment was made to Judas for his deed, even if the amount may not have been exactly 30 pieces of silver: "Although the report that his fee was 30 pieces of silver is dubious because, like so much else in this part of the Gospels, it is an echo of the scriptures, it is probable enough that Judas was paid for what he did."

Here are some mentions of the same sum, much earlier:

If the ox gore a bondman or a bondwoman, he shall give unto their master thirty shekels of silver, and the ox shall be stoned. (Exodus 21:32)

And I said unto them: "If ye think good, give me my hire; and if not, forbear." So they weighed for my hire thirty pieces of silver. And the Lord said unto me: "Cast it into the treasury, the goodly price that I was prized at of them." And I took the thirty pieces of silver and cast them into the treasury, in the house of the Lord. (Zechariah 11:12, 13)

305

The Travels of Paul

The apostle Paul was the individual most responsible for helping to create a worldwide Church. Below are listed the places visited by Paul during his four major journeys. Most of these cities issued coins in ancient times, and collectors are often fond of assembling sets of coins from the cities of Paul's journeys.

Paul's First Journey (Acts 13:1–14:28)

Antioch, Seleucis & Pierea
Salamis, Cyprus
Paphos, Cyprus
Perga, Pamphylia
Antioch, Pisidia
Iconium, Lycaonia
Lycaonia
Lystra, Lycaonia
Derbe, Lycaonia

Paul's Second Journey (Acts 15:36–18:22)

Antioch, Syria
Tarsus, Cilicia
Derbe, Lycaonia
Lystra, Lycaonia
Iconium, Lycaonia
Antioch, Pisidia
Troas
Neapolis, Macedon
Philippi, Macedon
Thessalonica, Macedon
Beroea, Macedon
Athens, Attica
Corinth, Corinthia
Ephesus, Ionia
Paphos, Cyprus
Caesarea, Samaria
Jerusalem, Judaea

Paul's Third Journey (Acts 18:23–21:16)

Antioch, Seleucis & Pierea
Iconium, Lycaonia
Ephesus, Ionia
Thessalonica, Macedon
Corinth, Corinthia
Philippi, Macedon
Miletus, Ionia
Rhodes
Paphos, Cyprus
Tyre, Phoenecia
Ptolemais, Phoenecia
Caesarea, Samaria
Jerusalem, Judaea

Paul's Voyage to Rome (Acts 15:36–18:22)

Caesarea, Samaria
Sidon, Phoenecia
Myra, Lycia
Crete
Malta
Syracuse, Sicily
Rhegium, Bruttium
Puteoli, Italy
Rome, Italy

APPENDIX A

Conversion Table Between Common References
On Jewish Coins

Hendin	AJC	Meshorer	Reifenberg
1	I,116,8	X	—
1a	I,116,9	—	—
2	I,115,4	1	—
2a	I,115,2	1a	—
3	I,116,10	2	—
3a	I,116,12	—	—
4	I,115,1	4	—
5	I,117,6	—	—
5a	I,117,15	—	—
5b	I,117,17b	—	—
6	I,160,1–3	—	—
7	I,Group A	5	16
8	I,Group B	6	17
9	I,Group D	7,7a	—
10	I,Group Ca	8	14
11	I,Group Cb	—	—
12	I,Group Cd	9	15
13	I,Group Ce	10	—
14	I,Group E	12	20
15	I,Group F	13	19
16	I,Group G	14	—
17	I,Group I	17,17a	18,18a
18	I,Group H	15	—
19	I,Group Hd	16	—
20	I,Group K	18	9
21	I,Group P	18a	—
22	I,Group M	19	8
23	I,Group N	20a	—
23a	I,Group N	—	—
24	I,Group N	20a	—
25	I,Group O	21a	—
26	I,Group S	22	11
27	I,Group S	23	—
28	I,Group T	24	—
29	I,Group R	25	7
30	I,Group L	26	10
31	I,Group Q	27	9a
32	I,Group Ja	28	13
33	I,Group Jb–Jc	29	—
34	I,Group U	30	21
35	I,Group V	31	22
36	I,Group Y	33	25

Conversion Table Between Common References
On Jewish Coins (continued)

Hendin	AJC	Meshorer	Reifenberg
37	I,Group W	34	—
38	I,Group Z	36	23
39	II,235,1	37	26
40	II,235,2	38	27
41	II,235,3	39	28
42	II,235,5	40	29
43	II,236,7	41a	30
44	II,236,10	42	32
45	II,236,11	43	—
46	II,236,12	—	—
47	II,236,13	—	—
48	II,237,14	46	—
49	II,237,15	47	—
50	II,237,15	49	—
51	II,237,18	50	35
52	II,238,19	51	—
53	II,238,20	52	—
54	II,237,17	53	33
55	II,237,17k	53c	—
56	II,238,23	54	34
57	II,238,22	55	36
58	II,239,1b	56	33a
59	II,239,2b	57	57
60	II,240,5	58	56
61	II,239,3	59a	53
62	II,240,4	60a	54
63	II,241,6	61	55
64	II,242,1	63	—
65	II,242,3	64	—
66	II,242,10	69	46a
67	II,242,12	70	47
68	II,243,17	74	50
68a	II,243,18	—	—
69	II,243,19	75	52
70	II,245,6	77	37
70a	II,244,1	—	—
71	II,243,3	78	38
71a	II,246,12	—	—
72	II,246,14	84	44
79	II,247,4	94	74
73	II,247,I	85	58
74	II,247,2	87	64
75	II,249,11	88	59
76	II,249,8	89	60
76a	II,248,5a	93b	—
76b	II,248,6	92	62

Conversion Table Between Common References
On Jewish Coins (continued)

Hendin	AJC	Meshorer	Reifenberg
77	II,Supp.IV,1	—	68
78	II,Supp.IV,5	—	71
80	II,250,2	96	78
81	II,250,4	98	75
82	II,250,5	99	76
83	II,250,6	100	77
84	II,256,38	106	84
85	II,256,17	112	89
86	II,255,32a	115	91
87	II,251,11	120	95
88	II,253,20	124	97
88a	II,253,21	—	—
89	II,253,22	127	99
90	II,253,23	129	101
91	II,254,28	130	102
92	II,254,29	131	—
93	II,256,42	135	108
94	II,256,43	136	109
95	II,255,36	142	—
96	II,255,35	143	106
97	II,258,52	145	117
98	II,258,53	146	113
99	II,258,56	147	116
100	II,Supp.V,1	216	118
101	II,Supp.V,3	217	119
102	II,Supp.V,1	218	120
103	II,Supp.V,5	219	121
104	II,Supp.V,6	220	122
105	II,Supp.V,8	221	123
106	II,Supp.V,10	222	124
107	II,Supp.V,12	223	125
108	II,Supp.V,16	224	127
109	II,Supp.V,15	225	126
110	II,Supp.V,17	226	128
111	II,Supp.V,18	227	129
112	II,Supp.V,19	228	130
113	II,Supp.V,21	229	131
114	II,Supp.V,23	230	132
115	II,Supp.V,24	231	133
116	II,Supp.V,32	232	134
117	II,Supp.V,29	233	135
118	II,Supp.V,35	234	136
119	II,259,3	148	137
120	II,259,6	149	138
120a	II,260,7	150	—
121	II,260,8	151	139

Conversion Table Between Common References
On Jewish Coins (continued)

Hendin	AJC	Meshorer	Reifenberg
122	II,260,10	152	140
123	II,260,12	153	147
123a	II,261,13c	153a	147a
124	II,261,18	154	141
125	II,261,19	155	142
126	II,261,20	156	148
126a	II,261,13c	—	—
127	II,262,23	158	143
128	II,262,25	159	144
129	II,262,27	161	4
130	II,262,29	162	5
131	II,262,30	163	6
131a	II,263,30d	163a	6a
132	II,263,31	164	145
133	II,264,1	165	163
134	II,267,17	167	169
135	II,264,4	168	191
136	II,264,3	169	190
137	II,265,5	170	193
137a	II,265,5c	—	—
138	II,270,40	171	194
139	II,265,6	172	192
140	II,265,7	173	189
141	II,265,10	175	195
142	II,268,20	176	171
143	II,267,19	177	172
144	II,267,13	180	165
145	II,266,12	178	—
146	II,267,16	181	164
147	II,268,26	182	174
148	II,268,33	183	173
149	II,268,28	184	—
150	II,268,24	185	—
151	II,268,21	186	—
152	II,268,25	187	178
153	II,268,23	188	177
154	II,269,31	189	179
155	II,269,36a	190	180
156	II,269,38	191	198
157	II,270,39	192	199
158	II,271,46	193	—
159	II,272,50	194	—
160	II,270,43a	195	200
161	II,271,49	198	202
162	II,272,51	199	167

Conversion Table Between Common References
On Jewish Coins (continued)

Hendin	AJC	Meshorer	Reifenberg
163	II,272,53	201	166
164	II,274,66	202	181
164a	II,275,67	202a	—
165	II,273,59b	203	182
166	II,274,62a	204	183
167	II,273,55a	205	184
168	II,273,56b	—	—
169	II,274,64	206	187
170	II,275,68	207	185
171	II,274,60	208	186
172	II,273,57b	209	188
173	II,278,74	211	204
174	II,276,77	212	205
175	II,276,79	213	203
176	II,276,80	214	207
177	II,276,81	215	206
178	—	—	—
179	—	—	—
180	II,Supp.VII,1	235	152
181	II,Supp.VII,2	236	155
182	II,Supp.VII,3	237	154
183	II,Supp.VII,5	238	153
184	II,Supp.VII,9	239	156
185	II,Supp.VII,10	240	157
186	II,Supp.VII,8	241	159
187	II,Supp.VII,6	242	160
188	II,Supp.VII,7	243	161
189	II,Supp.VII,5	244	162
190	II,Supp.VII,3	245	158
191	II,Supp.VII,2	246	—

B.C.E.	C.E.	Era of Augustus (commenced B.C. 27) on Coins of Procurators	Years of Tiberius on Coins of Procurators	Years of Antipas	Years of Philip II	Years of Agrippa I	Observations
4				1	1	· ·	Death of Herod I., and division of his Kingdom.
3				2	2		
2		28		3	3		
1		29		4	4		
		30					
	1	31		5	5 L.E.		
	2	32		6	6		
	3	33		7	7		
	4	34		8	8		
	5	35		9	9		
	6	36 L.ΛϚ		10	10	· ·	Archelaus deposed. Coponius first Procurator.
	7	37		11	11		
	8	38		12	12L.IB		
	9	39 L.ΛΘ		13	13		
	10	40 L.M		14	14	· ·	M. Ambivius succeeds Coponius.
	11	41 L.MA		15	15		
	12			16	16 L.IϚ		[Ambivius.
	13			17	17	· ·	Annius Rufus succeeds M.
	14		1	18	18	· ·	Death of Augustus. Tiberius Emperor. Valerius Gratus succeeds Annius Rufus.
	15		2 L.B	19	19 L.IΘ		
	16		3 L.Γ	20	20		
	17		4 L.Δ	21	21		
	18		5 L.C	22	22		
	19		6	23	23		
	20		7	24 L.KΔ	24		
	21		8	25	25		
	22		9	26	26		
	23		10	27	27		
	24		11 L.IA	28	28		
	25		12	29	29	· ·	Pontius Pilate succeeds Valerius Gratus.
	26		13	30	30 L.Λ		
	27		14 L.IΔ	31	31		
	28		15	32	32		
	29		16 L.IϚ	33L.ΛΓ	33 L.ΛΓ		
	30		17 L.IZ	34L.ΛΔ	34 L.ΛΔ		
	31		18 L.IH	35	35		
	32		19	36	36		
	33		20	37L.ΛZ	37 L.ΛZ		
	34		21	38	38	· ·	Death of Philip II.
	35		22	39	· ·	· ·	Pilate sent to Rome. Marcellus appointed by Vitellius.
	36		23	40			
	37		24	41		1 (and 2)	Death of Tiberius. Caligula.
	38			42		3	Marullus Procurator.
	39			43 L.MΓ		4	Antipas banished to Gaul.
	40					5 L.Є	

Chart from Madden, revised and updated.

C.E.	Years of Claudius on coins of Procurators.	Years of Nero on coins of Procurators.	Years of Agrippa I. continued.	AGRIPPA II.		Observations.
				Coins dated to the era of 56 CE, under Nero.	Coins dated to the era of 61 CE, under the Flavians.	
41	1		6 L.S	. .	. .	Caligula assassinated. Claudius.
42	2		7 L.Z			
43	3		8 L.H			
44	4		9 L.Θ	. .	. .	Death of Agrippa I. Cuspius Fadus, Procurator.
45	5					
46	6					
47	7	. .		. .	. .	Tiberius Alexander, Procurator.
48	8					
49	9			. .	. .	Ventidius Cumanus, Procurator.
50	10					Agrippa II. succeeded Herod, King of Chalcis.
51	11					
52	12			. .	. .	Claudius Felix, Procurator.
53	13 L.IΓ				. .	Chalcis taken away from Agrippa II. and the tetrarchy of Philip and Lysanias given to him instead.
54	14 L.IΔ	1			. .	Death of Claudius. Nero.
55		2			. .	Agrippa receives from Nero, the cities of Tiberias, Tarichæa and Julias.
56		3		1		
57		4		2		
58		5 L.Є		3		
59		6		4		
60		7		5 N.E	. .	Porcius Festus succeeds Felix as Procurator.
61		8		6	1	
62		9		7	2	Death of Festus. Annas Procurator.
63		10		8	3	Annas succeeded by Albinus.
64		11		9	4	
65		12		10 L.I	5	Gessius Florus, Procurator.
66		13		11 AI TOY	6	Jewish war begins.
67		14 L.IΔ		KAI ɯ	7	Capture of the city of Jotapata.
68		15			8	Death of Nero. Galba, Otho and Vitellius.
69					9	Vespasian Emperor. Titus & Domitian made *Cæsars*. [Vespasian.
70					10	
71					11	Conquest of Judæa. Cos. III. of
72					12	Cos. IV. of Vespasian. Cos. II. of
73					13	[Titus.
74					14 { ET.ΔI L.IΔ	
75					15 ET.IE	
76					16	
77					17	
78					18 ET.HI	
79					19 ET.IΘ	Death of Vespasian. Titus.
80					20	Cos. VIII. of Titus.
81					21	Death of Titus. Domitian.

C.E.	AGRIPPA II. continued. Coins dated to the era of 61 CE, under the Flavians (continued).	OBSERVATIONS.
82	22	
83	23	
84	24 ϜΤ.ΚΔ	Domitian surnamed *Germanicus*.
85	25 ΕΤ.ΚΕ	
86	26 ΕΤ.ΚϚ	Cos. XII. of Domitian. (12th consulship.)
87	27 ΕΤ.ΚΖ	
88	28	
89	29 ΕΤ.ΚΘ	
90	30 ΕΤ.Λ	
91	31	
92	32	
93	33	
94	34 ΕΤ.ΔΛ	
95	35 ΕΤ.ΕΛ	
96	36	Death of Domitian. Nerva.
97	37	
98	38	Death of Nerva. Trajan.
99	39	
100	40	Death of Agrippa II.
to		
114		
115	. .	Sedition of the Jews in Cyrene and Egypt.
116		
117	. .	Sedition suppressed by Lusius Quietus.
118		Death of Trajan. Hadrian.
to		
128	. .	Hadrian assumes the title of *Pater Patriæ*.
to		
131	. .	Foundation of *Ælia Capitolina*.
132	. .	Jewish war.
133		
134	. .	Severus sent from Britain to Judæa.
135	. .	Surrender of Bethar in Aug. and the war
to		ended soon after. Death of Bar-cochab.
138	. .	Death of Hadrian.

THE HEBREW LEGENDS.

EARLY SHEKELS AND HALF SHEKELS.

Obv.

1. ꓱ W ꓷ P Ɏ ∠ W Y ꓩ ꓱ

   ירושלם קדשה

   Jerushalem Kedoshah

   Holy Jerusalem.

   } First year shekels
   and
   half shekels.

2. ꓱ W Y ꓷ P ꓱ Ɏ ꓲ ∠ W Y ꓩ ꓱ

   ירושלים הקדושה

   Jerushalaim ha-Kedoshah

   Jerusalem the Holy.

   } The remaining
   years.

Rev.

3. ∠ F ꓩ W ꓩ ∠ P W

   שקל ישראל

   Shekel Israel

   Shekel of Israel.

   } Shekels.

4. ∠ ꓩ W ꓱ ꓩ ∠ ⊟

   חצי השקל

   Chatzi ha-Shekel

   Half-shekel.

   } Half shekels.

Numerals.

F = א · I: ꓯ · 2 · ꓶ · 2 . ꓶ · ꓶ · 3. 4 = ꓶ · 4 . ꓱ = ח · 5

W = שׁ preceding a numeral stands for

5. שׁנת = Shenath = year.

EARLY COPPER.

Obv.

6. Ɏ ꓶ ꓶ ꓩ X ∠ F ꓶ ∠

   לגאלת ציון

   Lig'ullath Zion

   Of the redemption of Zion.

   } on all modules.

Rev.

7. ꓩ ∠ ⊟ ꓷ ꓶ ꓶ F X Ɏ ω

   שׁנת ארבע הצי

   Shenath arba Chatzi

   In the fourth year, one half.

8. ꓷ ꓶ ꓶ ꓷ ꓶ ꓶ X X Ɏ ꓦ

   שׁנת ארבע רבוע

Shenath arba Rebia
In the fourth year, one quarter.

9. שנת ארבע
Shenath arba
In the fourth year.

___

HASHMONEAN FAMILY.

John Hyrcanus.
Rev.
10.

	יהו וחנן
	הכהו הג
	דל וחבר ה
	יהודים

Jehochanan Hakkohen Haggadol Vecheber Hajehudim.
John the High Priest and the Senate of the Jews.
Rev.
11.

	יהוכ
	בג חכהן
	הגדל וה
	בר חיה
	דים

Jehokanan Hakkohen Haggadol Vecheber Hajehudim
John the High Priest and the Senate of the Jews.
Rev.
12.

	יהוכ
	ננהכהן ה
	גדל ראש
	חברהיה
	דים

Jehokanan Hakkohen Haggadol Rosh Cheber Hajehudim.
John the High Priest, Chief of the Senate of the Jews.

JUDAS ARISTOBULUS.

Rev.
13.

	יהוד
	הכהןהגד
	ור יחבר
	היהודים

Jehudah Hakkohen Haggadol Vecheber Hajeduhim.
Judas the High Priest and Senate of the Jews.

ALEXANDER JANNAEUS.

Obv.

14.   𐤉𐤄𐤅𐤍𐤕𐤍 𐤄𐤌𐤋𐤊

יהונתן המלך

Jehonathan Hammelek.
Jonathan The King.

Rev.

15.   𐤉𐤍𐤕𐤆   יניתז
       הכהן ה
       גדל וחבר
       היהדים

Jonathan Hakkohen Haggadol Vecheber Hajehudim.
Jonathan the High Priest and Senate of the Jews.

Rev.

16.   𐤉𐤄𐤅   יהו
       .....𐤍𐤕𐤍   נתן..
                    . . . . .
                    . . . . .

Jehonathan &c.
Jehonathan (or Jonathan) &c.

Obv.

17.   𐤉𐤄𐤅𐤍𐤕𐤍 𐤄𐤌𐤋𐤊

יהונתן המלך

Jehonathan Hammelek.
Jonathan the King

ALEXANDRA.

Rev.

18.   𐤕? 𐤗 = ת   and other letters, perhaps

       𐤋𐤊𐤕𐤀𐤅   = מלכתא = Queen

ALEXANDER II.

Rev.

19.   𐤃𐤋𐤔𐤃𐤓𐤉𐤔𐤋𐤏   עלצדר(עש) גדל

Alexandras Gadol.
Alexander great (high Priest).

ANTIGONUS.

Obv.

20.   𐤌𐤕𐤕𐤉𐤄 𐤄𐤊𐤄𐤍 𐤄𐤂𐤃𐤋 𐤅𐤄𐤁𐤓 𐤄𐤉𐤄𐤅𐤃𐤉𐤌

מתתיה הכהן הגדל והבר היהודים

Mattathiah Hakkohen Haggadol Vecheber Hajehudim.
Matthias the High Priest and Senate of the Jews.

Ⴕ Ⴎ   אש. = First year.

ⴑ Ⴎ   שב. = Second year.

FIRST REVOLT.
Obv.

21.   Ⴘ ⵣ X W   X Ⴝ W   שנת שתים

Shenath shtayim. Year two.

22.   W Ⴘ ⵏ W   X Ⴝ W   שנת שלוש

Shenath shalosh. Year three.
Rev.

23.   Ⴝ Ⴕ ⵣ Ⴔ   X ⴺ Ꟑ   חרות ציון
Cheruth Zion
Deliverance of Zion

SECOND REVOLT.
Obv.

24.   ⵏ Ⴣ Ⴄ Ⴣ Ⴗ ⵏ ⴺ L Ⴕ   אלעזר הכהן

(usually retrograde).
Eleazar Hakkohen.
Eleazar the Priest.

25.   Ⴘ Ⴕ Ⴃ Ⴘ W   שמעון
         Ⴕ Z W Ⴝ   נשיא
         ⵏ Ⴕ Ⴘ W Ⴟ   ישראל

Shimoun Nasi Israel.
Simon Prince of Israel.

26.
    or ⵅ Ⴘ O Ⴘ W   שמעו (for שמעון.)
         Ⴘ ⵅ O Ⴘ W

Shimoun.
Simon.

27.   Ⴘ ⵏ Ⴍ Ⴟ Ⴕ Ⴘ Ⴟ   ירושלם

Jerushalem.
Jerusalem.
Rev.

28.   ⵏ Ⴕ Ⴘ Ⴍ Z   X ⵏ Ⴔ Ⴟ ⵏ   X ꟐႵ   X Ⴝ Ⴍ

שנת אחת לגאלת ישראל

Shenath achath Lige'ullath Israel
First year of the redemption of Israel

29. ⌐⊦9ω⥾ [X⊬]9B⌐9W

שב לחר]ות[ישראל

Schin Beth. Lecheruth Israel.
Second year of the deliverance of Israel.

30. 𐤉⌐ω⼂9⥾ X⼂9BⱢ   לחרות ירושלם

Lecheruth Jerushalem.
Of the deliverance of Jerusalem.

   * In the above table the legends are in all cases completed, but the legends on the coins themselves are not only often incomplete but blundered ; and the letters sometimes, if they are all on the coins, present impossible forms of words.

   The formation of the letters is often carelessly achieved ; so that the argument from epigraphy is a precarious one. Generally speaking the letters are more carefully formed upon the silver coins and copper of larger modules. It seems almost as if there were two scripts, as is the case with Marathi — the one official and particular, the other of a more cursive character and considerably variant in form.

GREEK LEGENDS.

HASHMONEAN FAMILY

Time of John Hyrcanus.

31. **ΒΑΣΙΛΕΩΣ ΑΝΤΙΟΧΟΥ ΕΥΕΡΓΕΤΟΥ.**
[Money of] King Antiochus the Benefactor (Antiochus VII of Syria). Two dates.
ΑΠΡ. = Era of Seleucidae 181 = B.C. 132.
ΒΠΡ. =   —   182 = B.C. 131.

Alexander Jannaeus.

32. Rev. **ΒΑΣΙΛΕΩΣ ΑΛΕΞΑΝΔΡΟΥ.**
[Money of] King Alexander.

Alexandra.

33. **ΒΑΣΙΛΙΣ ΑΛΕΣΑΝΔ.**
[Money of] Queen Alexandra.

Antigonus.

34. Rev. **ΒΑΣΙΛΕΩΣ ΑΝΤΙΓΟΝΟΥ.**
[Money of] King Antigonus.

HEROD FAMILY

Herod the Great.

35. **ΒΑΣΙΛΕΩΣ ·ΗΡΩΔΟΥ.**
[Money of] King Herod.
Date **LΓ** = year three.
Ϸ τρίχαλκον = Three chalcoi.

Herod Archelaus.

36. **ΗΡΩ ΔΟΥ ΕΘΝΑΡΧΟΥ.**
[Money of] Herod the Ethnarch.

Herod Antipas.

37. Obv. **ΗΡΩΔΟΥ ΤΕΤΡΑΡΧΟΥ.**
[Money of] Herod the Tetrarch.
Dates **L ΜΓ** or **L ΜΔ** year 43 or 44 or **ΕΤΟ[ΥΣ] ΜΓ** of the
year 43.

38. Rev. **ΤΙΒΕΡΙΑC.**
Tiberias (on Lake Gennesareth).

39. Rev. **ΓΑΙΩ ΚΑΙCΑΡΙ ΓΕΡΜΑΝΙΚΩ ΣΕΒ[ΑΣΤΙ].**
In the reign of Caius Caesar Germanicus Augustus.

40. Obv. **ΚΑΙCΑΡΙ CΕΒΑCΤU** (*sic*).
In the reign of Augustus Caesar.

41. Obv. **ΤΙΒΕΡΙΟC CΕΒΑCΤΟC ΚΑΙCΑΡ.**
[Money of] Tiberius Augustus Caesar.

42. Rev. **ΦΙΛΙΠΠΟΥ ΤΕΤΡΑΡΧΟΥ.**
[Money of] Philip the Tetrarch.
Reverse bears date.
L ΙΒ = year 12.
L ΙΣ = — 16.
L ΙΘ = — 19.
L ΛΓ = — 33.
L ΛΖ = — 37.

Herod Agrippa I.

43. Obv. **ΒΑCΙΛΕΩC ΑΓΡΙΠΑ.**
[Money of] King Agrippa.
Rev. **L S** = year 6.

PROCURATORS.

44. Obv. **ΚΑΙCΑΡΟC.**
Money of Caesar.
Rev. **L ΛΓ** = year 33. Coponius
　　 L ΛC = — 36.
　　 L ΛΘ = — 39. } Marcus Ambivius
　　 L Μ = — 40. } Annius Rufus.
　　 L ΜΑ = — 41.

Valerius Gratus.

45. Obv. **ΙΟΥΛ-CΕΒ.**
[Money of] Julia Augusta.

46. **KAICAP.**
[Money of] Caesar.

47. **TIBEPIOY.**
[Money of] Tiberius.

48. **TIB·KAICAP.**
[Money of] Tiberius Caesar.

49. **TIBEPIOY KAICAPOC.** With date **L·IS**=year 16.
[Money of] Tiberius Caesar.

50. Rev. **TIB.**
[Money of] Tiberius.

51. **KAICAP.**
[Money of] Caesar.

52. **IOYΛIA.**
[Money of] Julia.

53. **IOYΛIA KAICAPOC.**
[Money of] Julia Augusta.
Dates. **L Γ** year 3.
   L Δ year 4.
   L E — 5.
   L IA — 11.
   L IS — 16.
   L IZ — 17. } Pontius Pilate.
   L IH — 18.

Claudius Felix.

54. Obv. **TI KΛAYΔIOC KAICAP ΓEPM.**
[Money of] Titus Claudius Caesar Germanicus.

55. **NEPⲰ KΛAY KAICAP.**
[Money of] Nero Claudius Caesar.

56. Rev. **IOYΛIA AΓPIΠΠINA.**
[Money of] Julia Agrippina.

57. **BPIT·KAI.**
[Money of] Britannicus Caesar.
Date. **L IΔ.** Year 14.

58. *Porcius Festus.*
Obv. **L E KAICAPOC.**
Year 5 [Money of] Caesar.

59. Rev. **NEPⲰNOΣ.**
[Money of] Nero.

AFTER FIRST REVOLT.

Roman money commemorating Victory.
Vespasian.

60. Obv. **AYTOKP OYEΣΠ KAI ΣEB.**
[Money of] the Emperor Vespasian Caesar Augustus.

61. Rev. **IOYΔAIAϵ EAΛѠKYIAϹ**.
On the conquest of Judaea.

Titus.

62. Rev. **AYTOKP TITOϵ KAIϹAP ϹEB**.
[Money of] the Emperor Titus Caesar Augustus.

63. Rev. **IOYΔAIAϹ· EAΛѠKYIAϹ**.
On the Conquest of Judaea.

LATIN LEGENDS.

Vespasian.

64. Obv. IMP.CAES.VESPASIANVS.AVG :
Imperator Caesar Vespasianus Augustus.
The Emperor Caesar Vespasian Augustus.

65. TP.P.
Tribunitia Potestate. With the Tribunitian power.

66. P.M. or PONT.MAX.
Pontifex Maximus. Chief Priest.

67. COS.
Consul(followed by numeral indicating the year of the Consulate).

68. P.P.
Pater Patriae. His Country's Father.

69. CENS or CENSOR.
Censor.

70. DIVVS AVGVSTVS VESPASIANVS.
The Divine Augustus Vespasian (issued on his death and consequent deification).

71. Rev. VICT.AVG. or VICTORIA AVGVSTI.
Victoria Augusti.
The Victory of Augustus.

72. IVDAEA CAPTA, or sometimes IVDAEA only, or IVD CAP.
The captivity of Judaea.

73. IVDAEA DEVICTA.
The conquest of Judaea.

74. DE IVDAEIS.
In the matter of the Jews.

75. EX.S.C.
Ex Senatus consulto.
By command of the Senate.

76. TRIVMP.AVG.
Triumphus Augusti.

The triumph of Augustus.

77. VICTORIA NAVALIS.
The naval victory.

Titus.

78. Obv. IMP.T.CAESAR VESPASIANVS.
TR.POT.AVG.P.M.COS.P.P.CENSOR exactly the same as above but T stands for Titus.

79. AVG.F is Augusti Filius — the son of Augustus.
Rev. Similar legends to Vespasian except:

80. IVDAEA NAVALIS.
Judaea sea conquered.

Domitian.

81. Obv. IMP.CAES.DOMIT.AVG.GERM.
Imperator Caesar Domitianus Augustus Germanicus, with offices as Vespasian and Titus.

82. Rev. VICTOR AVG.
Victoria Augusti.
The Victory of Augustus.

Nerva.

83. Obv. IMP.NERVA CAES.AVG.P.M.TR.P.COS.III P.P.

The emperor Nerva, Caesar, Augustus, Chief Priest endowed with the Tribunitian Power, Consul for the third time, Father of his country.

84. Rev. FISCI IVDAICI CALVMNIA SVBLATA.
[To commemorate] the removal of the scandal of the Jewish Tax.

Hadrian.

85. Obv. HADRIANVS.AVG.COS.III.P.P.
Hadrianus Augustus Consul III Pater patriae.
Hadrian Augustus Consul for the third time, his country's Father.

86. Rev. ADVENTVI AVG.IVDAEAE.
[To commemorate] the arrival of Augustus in Judaea.

87. S.C.IVDAEA.
By command of the Senate. Judaea.

HEBREW ALPHABET & EQUIVALENTS.

Name.	Form.	Sound.	General Coin Form [1].	Number.
Aleph	א	Smooth breathing	☰ Ӿ ⨲	1
Beth	ב	B	⅃	2
Gimel	ג	G	ꓘ	3
Daleth	ד	D	◿	4
He	ה	H	⅊ ⊐	5
Vau	ו	V	⸚ ⅄ ⅀ ☓	6
Zayin	ז	Z	ⴸ ꟼ	7
Heth	ח	H	⊟	8
Teth	ט	Ṭ	none	9
Yodh	י	Ẏ	Z Z	10
Kaph	כ ך	K	ꓮ	20
Lamedh	ל	L	∠	30
Mem	מ ם	M	⸽	40
Nun	נ ן	N	⊿	50
Samekh	ס	S	none	60
Ayin	ע	Aspirate	◇	70
Pe	פ	P	none	80
Çadha	צ	SS	⚡	90
Qoph	ק	Q	ꟼ	100
Resh	ר	R	ꟼ	200
Shin	ש	SH	W ⊔ W	300
Tau	ת	T	✕	400

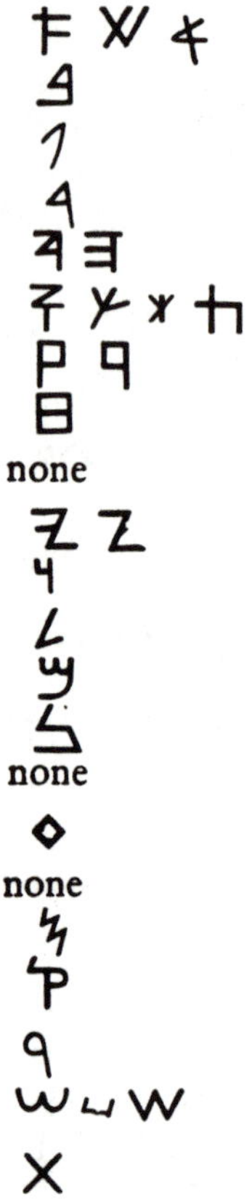

Short [2] Vowels { pâthaḥ ⎺ *a* as in fat   ḥîreq ⎺ *i* as in pin   qibbûç ⸛ *u* as in put
ṣᵉghôl ⸚ *e* as in pen   qámeç ḥaṭûph �⎺ *o* as in on

---

1. The coin forms are only general : most letters present variations.
2. The Hebrews used no vowel signs : a much later invention gives the above, placed under the letter.

GREEK ALPHABET & EQUIVALENTS.

Name.	Form.	Sound.	General Coin Form.	Number.
Alpha	A	A	A ⋀	1
Beta	B	B	B	2
Gamma	Γ	G	Γ	3
Delta	Δ	D	Δ	4
Epsilon	E	E	E ε	5
Zeta	Z	Z	I	7
Eta	H	EE	H	8
Theta	Θ	TH	Θ	9
Iota	I	I	I	10
Kappa	K	K	K	20
Lamda	Λ	L	Λ	30
Mu	M	M	M	40
Nu	N	N	N	50
Xi	Ξ	X	Ξ	60
Omicron	O	O (short)	O	70
Pi	Π	P	Π	80
Rho	P	R	P	100
Sigma	Σ	S	Σ C Ϲ	200
Tau	T	T	T	300
Upsilon	Υ	U	Y	400
Phi	Φ	PH	Φ	500
Chi	X	CH	X	600
Psi	Ψ	PS	Ψ	700
Omega	Ω	O long	Ω ω	800

1. The aspirate at the beginning of a word is represented by an inverted comma thus ό = ho.

2. The sign for 6 is Ϛ (*stigma*), an obsolete *vau*: for 90 is Ϙ, an obsolete *koppa* so the sign for 900 is Ϡ (*san*).

A thousand is written ϡ.

Numerals are often preceded by the sign Ⳑ : or the word ΕΤΟΥΣ.

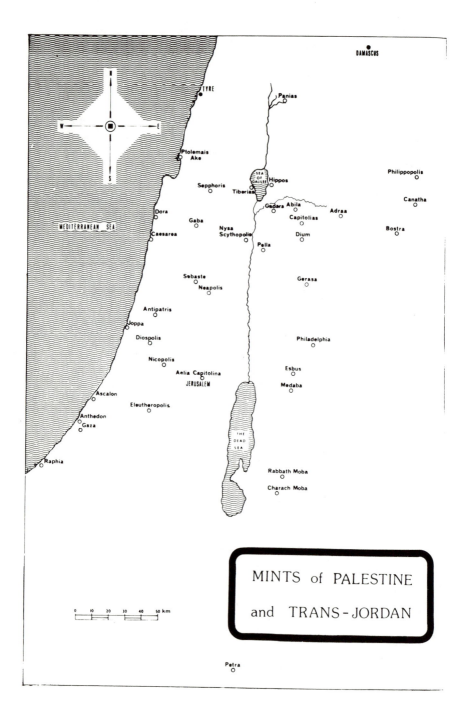

MINTS of PALESTINE and TRANS-JORDAN

Classical name of the city	Greek name of the city	Hebrew name of the city	Arabic name of the city	year of the local era	the first/Earliest date on the coins	Latest date on the coins	Last ruler on the coins	
1 Caesarea Paneas	KAICAPIA ΠANEAC	פניאס	بانياس	B.C. 4	POB=172	CKΓ=223	Elagabalus	218-222
2 Ptolemais Akko	ΠTOΛEMAIC AKH	עכו	عكا	B.C. 49	E = 5	COZ=277	Gallienus	253-268
3 Tiberias	TIBEPIAC	טבריה	طبريه	A.D. 19	IΘ = 19	C=200	Elagabalus	218-222
4 Sepphoris Diocaesarea	CEΠΦΩPIC ΔIOKAICAPEIA	צפורי	صفوريه	B.C. 61	IP=110	COΘ=279	Elagabalus	218-222
5 Dora	ΔΩPA	דור/דאר	الطنطوره	B.C. 64	A = 1	COE=275	Elagabalus	218-222
6 Gaba	ΓABA	גבע	الحارثيه	B.C. 61	IP=110	COΘ=279	Elagabalus	218-222
7 Caesarea	KAICAPIA	קיסריה	قيساريه				Volusianus	251-253
8 Nysa Scythopolis	NYCA CKYΘOΠOΛIC	בית-שאן	بيسان	B.C. 64	H = 8	ΤΔ=304	Volusianus	251-253
9 Sebaste, Samaria	CEBACTH	שומרון	سبسطيه	B.C. 25	PΘ =109	CKς=226	S.Alexander	222-235
10 Neapolis	NEAΠOΛIC	שכם	نابلس	A.D. 72	IA = 11	4 = 90	Volusianus	251-253
11 Antipatris	ANTIΠATPIC	אנטיפטריס	رأس العين				Elagabalus	218-222
12 Joppa	IOΠΠH	יפו	يافا				Elagabalus	218-222
13 Diospolis	ΔIOCΠOΛIC	לוד	اللد				S.Alexander	222-235
14 Nicopolis, Emmaus	NIKOΠOΛIC	עמאוס	عمواس	A.D. 219	IΘ = 19		Elagabalus	218-222
15 Aelia Capitolina		ירושלים	القدس				S.Alexander	222-235
16 Ascalon	ACKAΛΩN	אשקלון	عسقلان	B.C. 104	ς = 6	TΛH=338	Maximinus I	235-238
17 Eleutheropolis	EΛEYΘEPOΠOΛIC	בית-גוברין	بيت جبرين	A.D. 199	Γ = 3	IΘ= 19	Gordian III	238-244
18 Anthedon	ANΘHΔΩN	אנתדון	تيده	A.D. 219	Γ = 3	Z= 7	S.Alexander	222-235
19 Gaza	ΓAZA	עזה	غزه	B.C. 61	A = 1	TΔ=303	Gordian III	238-244
20 Raphia	PAΦIA	רפיח	رفح	B.C. 61	CΛZ=237	TΔ=304	Philip I	244-249
21 Philippopolis	ΦIΛIΠΠOΠOΛIC	פיליפופוליס	شهبا				Philip I	244-249
22 Hippos	IΠΠOC	סוסיתא	قلعة الحصن	B.C. 64	Kς = 26	CΠE=285	Elagabalus	218-222
23 Canatha	KANATA - KANAΘA	קנת	القنوات	B.C. 64	A = 1	CNΓ=253	Elagabalus	218-222
24 Abila	ABIΛA	אבל	تل أبيل	B.C. 64	CKς=227	CΠB=282	Elagabalus	218-222
25 Gadara	ΓAΔAPA	גדר	أم قيس	B.C. 64	A = 1	TΓ=303	Gordian III	238-244
26 Capitolias	KAΠITΩΛIAC	בית-ראש	بيت راس	A.D. 98	ΞH = 68	PKB=122	Gordian III	238-244
27 Adraa	AΔPAH	אדרעי	درعا	A.D. 105		PNA=151	Gallienus	253-268
28 Bostra	BOCTPA	בצרה	بصرى	A.D. 105	Oς = 76	PΔ=104	Traj.Decius	249-251
29 Dium	ΔION	דיון	تل الأشعري	B.C. 64	CΞH=268	CΠΓ=283	Elagabalus	218-222
30 Pella	ΠEΛΛA	פחל	طبقة فحل	B.C. 64	PME=145	CΠΓ=283	Elagabalus	218-222
31 Gerasa	ΓEPACA	גרש	جرش				Elagabalus	218-222
32 Philadelphia	ΦIΛAΔEΛΦIA	רבת-עמון	عمان	B.C. 64	PΛ =130	CΠA=281	Elagabalus	218-222
33 Esbus	ECBOYC	חשבון	حسبان	B.C. 64	PMA=141	CKZ=227	Elagabalus	218-222
34 Medaba	MHΔABA	מידבא	مادبا	A.D. 105	PA=101	PE=105	Elagabalus	218-222
35 Rabbath Moba	PABBAΘ MΩBA	רבת-מואב	الربه	A.D. 105	PΔ =104	PE=105	Elagabalus	218-222
36 Charach Moba	XAPAX MΩBA	כרך-מואב	الكرك	A.D. 105		PE=105	Elagabalus	218-222
37 Petra	ΠETPA	פטרה	البتراء	A.D. 105	KΘ = 29	Λ= 30	Elagabalus	218-222

BIBLIOGRAPHY

Barag, Dan. "The Countermarks of the Legio Decima Fretensis." In *Proceedings of the International Numismatic Convention* (Jerusalem, 26–31 December, 1963), pp. 9–11, 117–25. Jerusalem: Schocken, 1967.

Bartlett, John. *The First and Second Books of The Maccabeds; The Cambridge Bible Commentary.* Cambridge: Cambridge University Press, 1973.

Brauer, G. *Judaea Weeping.* New York: Crowell, 1970.

L. F. J. C. de Saulcy. *Numismatique de la Terre Sainte; description des monnaies autonomes et imperiales de la Palestine et de l'Arabie Petree.* Paris: J. Rothschild, 1874.

The Dating and Meaning of Ancient Jewish Coins and Symbols. Jerusalem: Israel Numismatic Society, 1958.

Encyclopedia Judaica, vols. 2–16, 1971; Vol. 1, 1972.

Grant, M. *Herod the Great.* New York: American Heritage, 1971.

——. *The Jews in the Roman World.* New York: Scribner's, 1973.

Hendin, D. *Guide to Ancient Jewish Coins.* New York: Attic Books, 1976.

Hill, G. F. *Catalogue of Greek Coins of Palestine.* (Reprint of 1914 edition). Bologna: Forni, 1965.

——. *Catalogue of Greek Coins of Phoenecia.* (Reprint of 1910 edition). Bologna: Forni, 1965.

Holy Scriptures According to the Masoretic Text. Philadelphia: The Jewish Publication Society of America, 1917, 1945.

Jeselsohn, D. "A New Coin Type with Hebrew Inscription." *Israel Exploration Journal,* XXIV (1974), p. 77.

Josephus, The Jewish War.

Kadman, Leo. *The Coins of Caesarea Maritima.* (Corpus Nummorum Palaestinensium). Jerusalem: Schocken, 1957.

——. *The Coins of Aelia Capitolina.* (Corpus Nummorum Palaestinensium). Jerusalem: Schocken, 1956.

——. *The Coins of the Jewish War.* (Corpus Nummorum Palaestinensium). Jerusalem: Schocken, 1960.

——. *The Coins of Akko Ptolemais.* (Corpus Nummorum Palaestinensium). Jerusalem: Schocken, 1961.

Kanael, B. "Ancient Jewish Coins and their Historical Importance. *Biblical Archaeology,* XXVI (1963), p. 38.

——. "The Greek Letters and Monograms on the Coins of Jehohanan the High Priest." *Israel Exploration Journal,* II (1952), p. 190.

——. "The Beginning of Maccabean Coinage." *Israel Exploration Journal,* I (1950), p. 170.

Kindler, A. *The Coins of Tiberias.* Tiberias: Hamei Tiberia, 1961.

——. *Coins of the Land of Israel.* Jerusalem: Ketter, 1974.

King James Version of The Holy Bible. New York: American Bible Society.

Madden, F. W. *History of Jewish Coinage and of Money in the Old and New Testament.* London: Quaritch, 1864.

Maltiel-Gerstenfeld, J. *260 Years of Ancient Jewish Coins.* Tel Aviv: Kol, 1982.

Mattingly, H. *Coins of the Roman Empire in the British Museum,* Vol. II. London: British Museum, 1966.

Mattingly, H., and Sydenham, E. *The Roman Imperial Coinage,* Vol. II. London: Spink and Son, 1968.

Meshorer, Y. *Ancient Jewish Coinage I and II.* New York: Amphora Books, 1982.

——. "A New Type of YHD Coin." *Israel Exploration Journal,* XVI (1966), p. 217.

——. *City Coins of Eretz-Israel and the Decapolis.* Jerusalem: Israel Museum, 1985.

——. *Production of Coins in the Ancient World.* Jerusalem: Israel Museum, 1970.

——. *Jewish Coins of the Second Temple Period.* Tel Aviv: Am Hasefer, 1967.

———. *Coins of the Ancient World.* Minneapolis: Lerner, 1974.

Mildenberg, L. *The Coinage of the Bar Kokhba War.* Salzburg: Verlag Sauerlander, 1984.

Mishnah. Oxford: Oxford University Press, 1933.

Naveh, J. "Dated Coins of Alexander Jannaeus." *Israel Exploration Journal,* XVIII (1968), p. 20.

Perlman, Moshe. *The Maccabees.* New York: Macmillan, 1973.

Price, M., and Trell, B. *Coins and Their Cities.* Detroit: Wayne State, 1977.

Rahmani, L. Y. "Silver Coins of the Fourth Century B.C. from Tel Gamma." *Israel Exploration Journal,* XXI (1971), p. 158.

Reifenberg, A. *Ancient Jewish Coins.* Jerusalem, 1947.

Rogers, E. *A Handy Guide to Jewish Coins.* London: Spink & Son, 1914.

Rosenberger, M. *The Rosenberger Israel Collection,* vols. I–IV. Jerusalem, 1972–74.

Spijkerman, A. *The Coins of the Decapolis and Provincia Arabia.* Jerusalem: Franciscan Printing Press, 1978.

Sukenik, E. L. "More About the Oldest Coins of Judaea." *JPOS,* XV, (1935), p. 341.

———. *Paralipomena Palestinensia. JPOS,* XIV, p. 178.

Whiston, William. *The Complete Works of Flavius Josephus.* Chicago: Thompson & Thomas, 1899.

Yadin, Y. *Bar-Kochba.* New York: Random House, 1971.

———. *Massada.* London: Weidenfeld & Nicolson, 1966.

KEY TO THE WEIGHTS (PLATE 1)

Syrian-Phoenician Weights, Babylonian Standard, 14 to 11 centuries B.C.E.

1. 2 Shekel, bronze, with small rings to adjust weight. 15.11g.
2. 1½ Shekel, hematite. 11.36g.
3. ½ Shekel, hematite. 5.08g.
4. ⅓ Shekel, hematite, 3.55g.
5. ½ Shekel, hematite, 4.17g.

Egyptian Weights, 11 to 9 centuries B.C.E.

6. 1 Qedet, bronze fish. 9.14g.
7. 1 Qedet, bronze bull head. 6.53g.
8. 2 Shekel (Babylonian Standard), bronze frog, 16.20g.
9. 5 Qedet, bronze. 45.2g.

Jewish Weights, 9 to 7 centuries B.C.E.

10. 5 Gerah, limestone. 3.05g.
11. Beqa, limestone. 5.99g.
12. Nezef, limestone. 10.10g.
13. 1 Shekel, limestone. 11.21g.
14. 2 Shekel, limestone. 22.35g.

Phoenician Weight, 4 to 3 centuries B.C.E.

15. 1 Stater, bronze. 11.70g.

Roman Weights, 1 century B.C.E. to 2 century C.E.

16. 2 Unciae, lead. 54.33g.
17. 2 Unciae, bronze. 51.92g.

Byzantine Weights, 5 to 7 centuries C.E.

18. 2 Unciae, bronze. 52.61g.
19. 3 numismata, bronze. 13.26g.
20. 3 numismata, bronze. 7.92g. (Significant deviation.)
21. 1 Numisma, bronze. 4.21g.

Islamic Weights, 7 to 12 centuries C.E.

22. 1 Uqiya, bronze. 27.55g.
23. ½ Uqiya, bronze. 14.54g.
24. 5 Scipulum, bronze. 5.69g.
25. 2 Dinar, bronze. 8.56g.
26. ½ Dinar, bronze. 2.06g.

Weights are from Münz Zentrum Auction 32 and 45; and Kölner Münzkabinett 28.

Ancient weights may vary from actual standards due to innacuracies in manufacture of weights as well as encrustation or deterioration due to age.

REFERENCES FOR COINS IN THE PLATES

Coins shown in photographs are from the author's collection, except the following:

From Ancient Jewish Coinage by Ya'akov Meshorer, numbers 8, 21, 28, 29, 33, 38, 41, 51, 52, 74, 67, 69, 70, 70a, 71, 71a, 71b, 72, 73, 74, 76, 76a, 76b, 77, 78, 79, 80, 81, 82, 83, 85, 88, 89, 90, 92, 94, 95, 127, 128, 133, 135, 136, 141, 142, 143, 145, 150, 151, 155, 156, 157, 180, 190, 191.

Courtesy of Herbert Kreindler, number 132.

Most of the drawings are from Madden, 1864 and 1881 editions. Most City Coin drawings are from DeSaulcy, 1874. Additional drawings from Bayerii, 1781; Mary Blanchard; and drawings for this edition by John Lane.

Cover design by John Lane.

Plate 1

Plate 2

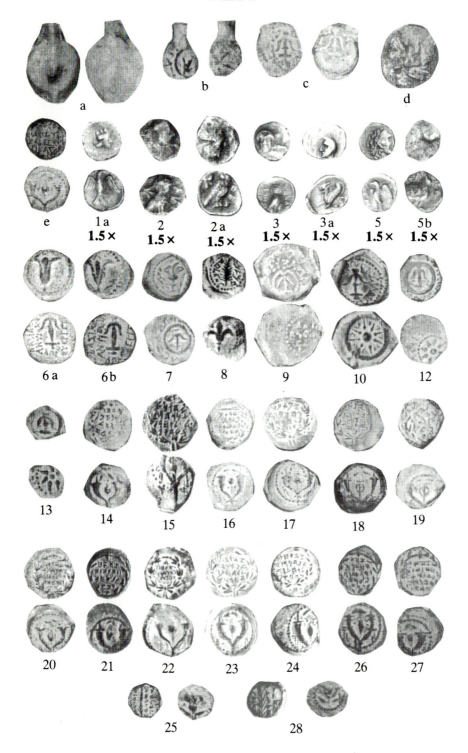

a

b

c

d

e

1 a
1.5×

2
1.5×

2 a
1.5×

3
1.5×

3 a
1.5×

5
1.5×

5 b
1.5×

6 a

6 b

7

8

9

10

12

13

14

15

16

17

18

19

20

21

22

23

24

26

27

25

28

Plate 3

30   31   32   33   36   37   38

29   34   35   39   40

41   42   43   44   45   46

47   48   49   51   52   53   54

Plate 4

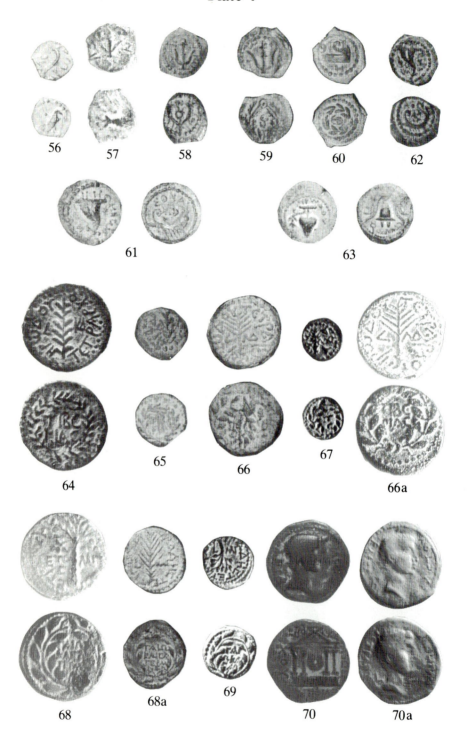

56 57 58 59 60 62

61 63

64 65 66 67 66a

68 68a 69 70 70a

Plate 5

71

71a

71b

72

72a

79

73

74

75

76

76a

76b

77

78

Plate 6

80   81   82   83

84   85

88   88a

86   87   89

90   91   92   93   94   95

Plate 7

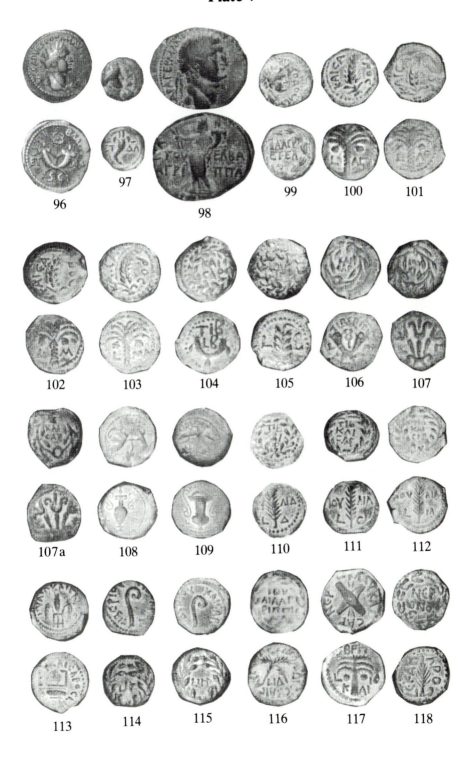

96

97

98

99 100 101

102 103 104 105 106 107

107a 108 109 110 111 112

113 114 115 116 117 118

Plate 8

119

120

122

121

123

126

124

125

128

127

129

132

130

131

Plate 9

133

134

135

137

136

137a

138

139

140

140b

140c

Plate 10

141

142

143

144

145

146

147

148

149

150

151

152

153

Plate 11

154

155

156

158

157

160

160 b

160 a

159

161

Plate 12

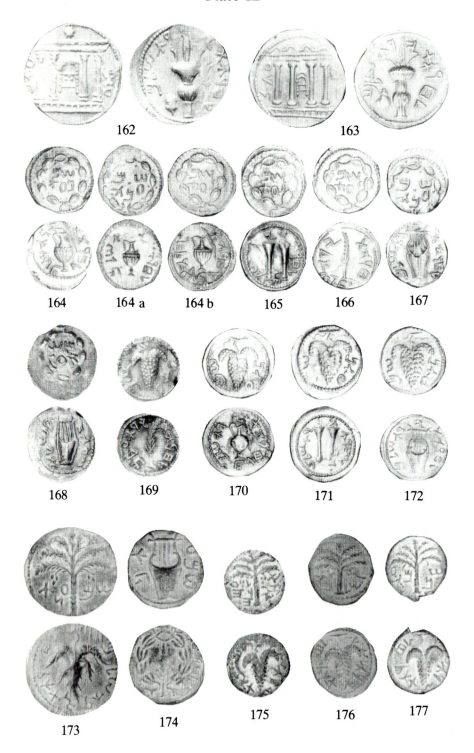

162

163

164

164 a

164 b

165

166

167

168

169

170

171

172

173

174

175

176

177

Plate 13

178   179   180   181   182

183   184   185   187

186   188   189   190   191

Plate 14

192   195   210

198   199   200

201   203   204

206   207   211

212   213   215

Plate 15

214 a

216

216 a

231

219

237

229

239

240

242

243

244

246

Plate 16

245

254

255

256

257

263

264

265

266

267

271

276

279

281